SALADS

MORE THAN 80 FRESH IDEAS

SALADS

MORE THAN 80 FRESH IDEAS

MURDOCH BOOKS

contents

toss it   6
salad know-how

poolside   12
cool salads to dip into

ladies who lunch   64
keeping it all lovely and light

lunchbox   108
power-packed for people on the go

warm winter   154
hot ideas for chilly days and nights

index   203

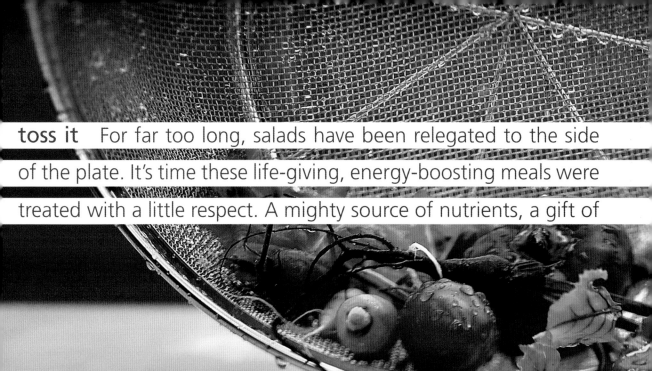

toss it For far too long, salads have been relegated to the side of the plate. It's time these life-giving, energy-boosting meals were treated with a little respect. A mighty source of nutrients, a gift of

nature's bounty, salads are blessed with virtues too numerous to list. For hot days, cold days, lunch with the gals or lunch on the run, nothing beats a salad, so look to your crisper and get tossing!

toss it

There is no better showcase for truly fresh produce than a salad, be it ripe tomatoes bursting with flavour, succulent prawns rich with the taste of the ocean, or crumbly, creamy feta with its salty, goaty tang. The joy of a great salad lies in celebrating all the pleasures of authentic ingredients in peak condition.

The versatility of salad is one of its greatest assets. When you need a simple meal that can be thrown together in an instant, a fresh, leafy ensemble full of crisp raw vegetables dressed with a classic vinaigrette is just the first option. There are infinite recipes for absolutely gorgeous salads that involve little more effort than some chopping and tossing, yet don't compromise on taste.

Sometimes, though, there's nothing quite so satisfying as rolling up your sleeves, taking over the kitchen and creating a complex, intricate meal offering sophisticated new flavours. Again, there is a salad to suit. Experimentation is one of the great joys of cooking, and salads offer enormous scope for innovation and discovery. Whatever taste you are seeking out, creating a dish with a real depth of flavour, or which somehow tastes fresh and new, is its own

reward. As just one example there are wonderfully intense Asian dressings that require dozens of ingredients, four different steps and a good half hour to prepare. The deeper pleasure of taking the time to create something rare and special, especially when you're cooking for others, is an experience just begging to be shared.

There is, of course, more to salad than sheer good taste. The benefits of eating fresh vegetables are so widely acknowledged that it would be redundant to point them out again. However, we sometimes forget the value of eating a wide variety of different foods. To satisfy your body's need for the full range of vitamins and minerals, eating vegetables alone is simply not enough. We also need to find a way to include nuts, dairy, meat, seafood, fruit, seeds, pulses and grains in our diet, both in the right balance and on a regular basis. Again, here is where the humble salad comes into its own, gathering an abundance of health-giving ingredients in ways that are limited only by your taste and your imagination. A rainbow of vegetables, slivers of salty ham, shavings of Parmesan cheese, a handful of nuts and a heap of leafy greens in the one meal is more than just a good start. And eating a variety of salads throughout the week is a **delicious** way of ensuring you meet all your dietary needs.

Of course, salads are also a **dieter's** best friend. Few of us have the discipline or willpower to be sensible all of the time. The weekend blow-out is a common feature of life, whether it's the slice of cake you **swore** you wouldn't have, or maybe those two extra glasses of wine you definitely shouldn't have had! So if you can't be good all of the time, the next **best** option is to be really good most of the time. Luckily, piling up on salad during the week is an excellent way to make sure those weekend lapses don't ruin all your hard work.

Presentation is an aspect of food that is all too often just an afterthought, yet when we eat, as with all the pleasures of the body, we are engaging all our **senses**. Taste and smell are obviously dominant, but there is an extra element of delight involved in eating a meal that looks **superb**. Happily, there is something innately appealing about a mound of fresh, colourful food **glistening** under a light coating of dressing.

The way you choose to plate up the meal is as important as the way you dress the table. While white plates are a definite classic, there is no need to limit yourself — don't be afraid to use colour on the table, especially when serving a salad. The jewel hues of raw vegetables, the soft creamy tones of cheese and the smoky notes of roast vegetables are all enhanced by a blast of colour on the table.

Many salads look wonderful heaped high on communal platters, and there's always something invitingly intimate about serving each other at the table. Other salads are better suited to individual plates and bowls, as the construction of the meal is part of its charm. However you choose to serve the meal, give free rein to your imagination when it comes to styling the table. Quirky accessories, sensuous fabrics and arresting colours can only enhance the pleasure of eating.

The key to it all is to keep the basics simple, then dress it up with your own individual touches that reflect your personal style. Seasonal food, fresh flavours and a burst of life-affirming colour are all you really need to create a memorable meal.

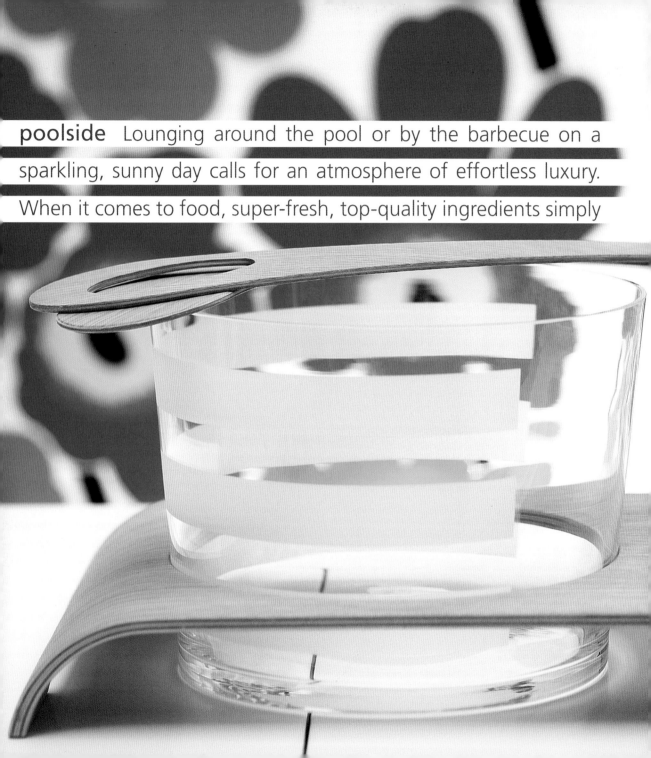

poolside Lounging around the pool or by the barbecue on a sparkling, sunny day calls for an atmosphere of effortless luxury. When it comes to food, super-fresh, top-quality ingredients simply prepared and beautifully presented are all you need to make a splash. A sizzling barbecue and a table laden with big bowls of salad set the scene for a perfect feast in the sun.

There is no better place to soak up the long days of summer than by the pool. Big umbrellas, banana lounges and a long, cool drink are some essential props and accessories that will create the right mood, but it's the food that sits at the heart of any event. Simple, light and fresh are the key qualities of summer eating and nothing quite fits the bill like a sensational selection of salads. Nobody wants to fill right up when they're frolicking by the water. It's not just about looking good in your swimming costume but about feeling satiated, yet still light and active. Salads are the ultimate in lightweight cuisine, but you can pack a heap of super flavours into a salad without a sense of having gone over the top, or you can keep it simple by going for a leafy base topped with one or two intense additions. Either way you've got the perfect combination for a party by the pool. Stylish entertaining without the stress is the mantra of poolside dining, and salads are the perfect way to achieve that balance between easy and elegant. Keeping it casual means you can relax and join in the fun, but there's no point in entertaining if you forget to make it special. Luckily it's so simple to achieve a feeling of plenty — just lay out a spread of delectable dishes and break open a loaf of crispy, crusty bread. When dishing up poolside, take your cue from the elements and go for a simple, effortless look that reflects the myriad blues of the water and sky, smartly accented with notes of crisp white. Cool patterns and unusual accessories help bring an eclectic modern edge to a timeless setting.

15

Slippery, slithery noodles hide a host of plump, sweet prawns in this crisp and nutty, light and lively salad.

prawn and rice noodle salad

250 g (9 oz) rice stick noodles
700 g (1 lb 9 oz) raw prawns
(shrimp), peeled and
deveined, tails intact
1 tbs olive oil
1 carrot, finely julienned
1 Lebanese (short) cucumber,
seeded and julienned
2 1/2 large handfuls coriander
(cilantro) leaves
80 g (2 3/4 oz/1/2 cup) roasted
unsalted peanuts, chopped

50 g (1 3/4 oz) crisp fried shallots
(see Note)

dressing
125 ml (4 fl oz/1/2 cup) rice
vinegar
1 tbs grated palm sugar
1 garlic clove, finely chopped
2 red chillies, finely chopped
3 tbs fish sauce
3 tbs lime juice
2 tbs peanut oil

Put the noodles in a large heatproof bowl, cover with boiling water and leave to soak for 10 minutes. Drain, rinse under cold water to cool, then drain again. Place in a large serving bowl.

Meanwhile, preheat a barbecue grill or chargrill pan (griddle) to high. Toss the prawns in the olive oil and cook for about 2–3 minutes, or until just opaque. Take them off the heat and toss them through the noodles with the carrot, cucumber and coriander.

To make the dressing, combine the vinegar, sugar and garlic in a small saucepan. Bring to the boil, then reduce the heat and simmer for 3 minutes to reduce slightly. Pour into a bowl and add the chilli, fish sauce and lime juice. Slowly whisk in the peanut oil, and season to taste.

Toss the dressing through the salad, scatter with the peanuts and crisp fried shallots and serve.

Note: Crisp fried shallots are red Asian shallot flakes used as a garnish in Southeast Asia. They are available from Asian food stores.

Serves 4

prawn and rice noodle salad

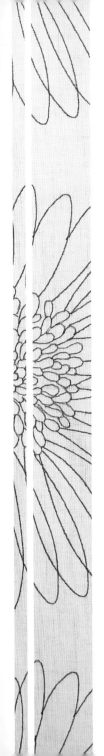

goat's cheese, avocado and smoked salmon salad

2 tbs extra virgin olive oil
1 tbs balsamic vinegar
40 g (1½ oz) baby rocket
    (arugula) leaves
1 avocado
100 g (3½ oz) smoked salmon
    pieces, sliced (see Note)

8 rounds of marinated goat's
    cheese, drained
2 tbs roasted hazelnuts,
    coarsely chopped

In a large bowl, whisk together the oil and vinegar and season to taste.

Cut the avocado lengthways into quarters, then discard the skin. Place an avocado quarter on each serving plate and arrange a small pile of rocket and smoked salmon over the top.

Stack two goat's cheese rounds on each plate and scatter the hazelnuts over the top. Drizzle the dressing over, season with a good grind of black pepper and serve at once.

Note: A whole smoked trout can be used instead of the salmon. Peel away the skin, remove the bones, then flake the flesh into bite-sized pieces.

Serves 4

marinated baby octopus salad

750 g (1 lb 10 oz) baby octopus
4 tbs olive oil
2 garlic cloves, crushed
1 red capsicum (pepper),
   thinly sliced

1 tbs sweet chilli sauce
2 tbs chopped coriander
   (cilantro)
2 tbs lime juice

Using a small, sharp knife, carefully cut between the head and tentacles of each octopus, just below the eyes. Grasp the body and push the beak out and up through the centre of the tentacles with your finger. Cut the eyes from the heads by slicing off a small disc. To clean the octopus heads, carefully slit through one side, avoiding the ink sac, and scrape out any gut from inside. Rinse well under running water and place in a large mixing bowl. Add the oil and garlic, mix well, then cover and marinate in the refrigerator for 1–2 hours.

When you're ready to eat, heat a barbecue grill or chargrill pan (griddle) to very hot. Cook the baby octopus, in batches if necessary, until just tender, about 3–5 minutes. Drain well on crumpled paper towels.

Put the capsicum, sweet chilli sauce, coriander and lime juice in a serving bowl, add the octopus and mix together. Serve warm or cold.

Serves 4

goat's cheese, avocado and smoked salmon salad

Roast beef is just sublime piled on spinach and lavishly dressed
with cool, creamy yoghurt laced with horseradish and lemon.

roast beef and spinach salad with horseradish cream

horseradish cream
125 g (4^1/$_2$ oz/^{1}/$_2$ cup) thick plain yoghurt
1 tbs creamed horseradish
2 tbs lemon juice
2 tbs cream
2 garlic cloves, crushed
a few drops of Tabasco sauce, or to taste

200 g (7 oz) green beans, trimmed
500 g (1 lb 2 oz) rump steak
1 red onion, halved
1 tbs olive oil
100 g (3^1/$_2$ oz) baby English spinach leaves
50 g (1^3/$_4$ oz/1^2/$_3$ cups) picked watercress leaves
200 g (7 oz) semi-dried (sun-blushed) tomatoes

To make the horseradish cream, whisk all the ingredients in a small bowl with a little black pepper to taste. Cover and chill for 15 minutes.

Bring a pot of lightly salted water to the boil, add the beans and blanch for 4 minutes, or until tender. Drain, refresh under cold water and drain again.

Meanwhile, preheat a griller (broiler) or barbecue hotplate to high. Brush the steak and onion halves with the oil. Cook the steak for 2 minutes on each side, or until seared but still rare, then remove from the heat, cover with foil and leave for 5 minutes. (Cook the beef a little longer if you prefer it medium or well done.) While the steak is resting, cook the onion for 2–3 minutes on each side, or until charred.

Toss the spinach, watercress, tomato and beans in a large salad bowl. Slice the beef thinly across the grain, then layer over the salad. Thinly slice the grilled onion, add to the salad and drizzle with the dressing. Season well with sea salt and freshly ground black pepper and serve.

Serves 4

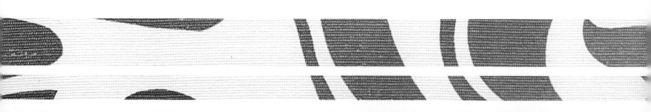

roast beef and spinach salad with horseradish cream

insalata caprese

3 large vine-ripened tomatoes, sliced
250 g (9 oz) bocconcini cheese, sliced (see Note)

16–20 whole basil leaves
3 tbs extra virgin olive oil

Arrange alternating slices of tomato and bocconcini on a serving platter. Slip the basil leaves in between the tomato and bocconcini slices. Drizzle with the oil, season well with salt and ground black pepper and serve.

Note: This popular salad is most successful when made with very fresh buffalo mozzarella, if you can find it. We've used bocconcini — small balls of fresh cow's milk mozzarella — in this recipe.

Serves 4 as a side salad

moroccan spiced carrot salad

2 cardamom pods
1 tsp black mustard seeds
1/2 tsp ground cumin
1/2 tsp ground ginger
1 tsp paprika
1/2 tsp ground coriander
35 g (1¹/4 oz/1/4 cup) currants
4 tbs olive oil
1 tbs lemon juice

2 tbs orange juice
4 carrots
2 large handfuls coriander
    (cilantro), finely chopped
2 tbs finely chopped pistachio
    nuts
1/2 tsp orange flower water
200 g (7 oz) thick plain yoghurt

Crush the cardamom pods to extract the seeds; discard the pods. Heat a frying pan over low heat and dry-fry the mustard seeds for a few seconds, or until they start to pop. Add the cardamom, cumin, ginger, paprika and ground coriander and cook for 10 seconds, or until fragrant. Remove from the heat and stir in the currants, oil, lemon juice and orange juice.

Peel and coarsely grate the carrots. Put the grated carrot in a large bowl, stir through the spice mixture, then cover and leave for 30 minutes. Toss through the chopped coriander, pile the salad onto a serving dish and sprinkle with the pistachios. Mix the orange flower water through the yoghurt and serve separately, for people to help themselves.

Serves 4 as a side salad

insalata caprese

grilled tofu with broccoli and sesame dressing

200 g (7 oz) broccoli, cut
  into florets
100 g (3¹/₂ oz) baby corn,
  halved lengthways
80 g (2³/₄ oz) snowpeas
  (mangetout), tailed
1 large red capsicum (pepper),
  sliced

200 g (7 oz) smoked tofu,
  cut into 5 mm (¹/₄ inch)
  thick slices

sesame dressing
3 tbs olive oil
2 tsp sesame oil
2 tbs lemon juice

Bring a pot of water to the boil and add a teaspoon of salt. Add the broccoli and cook for 30 seconds, then add the corn and snowpeas and cook for 1 more minute. Drain, refresh under cold water, then plunge into a bowl of cold water to cool. Drain well and toss in a serving dish with the capsicum.

Thoroughly whisk all the sesame dressing ingredients together in a small bowl. Pour half the dressing over the salad and gently toss to combine.

Heat a barbecue grill or chargrill pan (griddle) to medium. Add the tofu and cook for 2 minutes on each side, or until grill marks appear. Add to the salad with the remaining dressing, toss gently and serve.

Serves 4

red leaf salad

150 g (5¹/₂ oz) mixed red lettuce
    leaves (such as coral red
    lettuce or red leaf lettuce)
1 baby fennel bulb
    (about 100 g/3¹/₂ oz)
1 small red onion
2 tbs olive oil
1 tbs balsamic vinegar

Wash and dry the lettuce leaves, then tear them into bite-sized pieces.

Finely slice the fennel and onion and toss into a serving bowl with the shredded lettuce. Just before serving, drizzle the oil over the salad, then the vinegar. Toss lightly and serve.

Serves 4 as a side salad

grilled tofu with broccoli and sesame dressing

avocado and black bean salad

250 g (9 oz) dried black (turtle)
   beans
1 red onion, chopped
4 egg (Roma) tomatoes, chopped
1 red capsicum (pepper),
   chopped
375 g (13 oz) tinned corn
   kernels, drained
1 bunch coriander (cilantro),
   roughly chopped

2 avocados, chopped
1 mango, peeled and chopped
150 g (5^1/2 oz/1 bunch) rocket
   (arugula), leaves trimmed

lime and chilli dressing

1 garlic clove, crushed
1 small red chilli, finely chopped
2 tbs lime juice
3 tbs olive oil

Soak the beans in cold water overnight. Rinse well, drain and place in a large, heavy-based pot. Cover with cold water, bring to the boil, then reduce the heat and simmer for 1^1/2 hours, or until tender. Drain well and allow to cool slightly.

Put the beans in a large bowl with the onion, tomato, capsicum, corn, coriander, avocado, mango and rocket. Gently toss to combine.

Whisk all the lime and chilli dressing ingredients together in a small bowl. Pour over the salad, toss gently and serve.

Serves 4

radicchio with figs and ginger vinaigrette

1 radicchio lettuce
1 baby frisée (curly endive)
3 oranges (see Note)
1/2 small red onion, thinly
    sliced into rings
8 small green figs, quartered
3 tbs extra virgin olive oil

1 tsp red wine vinegar
1/8 tsp ground cinnamon
2 tbs orange juice
2 tbs very finely chopped glacé
    ginger, with 2 tsp syrup
2 pomegranates (optional),
    sliced in half

Wash the radicchio and frisée leaves thoroughly and drain well. Tear any large leaves into bite-sized pieces and toss in a salad bowl.

Peel and segment the oranges, discarding all the bitter white pith. Add to the salad leaves with the onion and figs, reserving eight fig quarters. Whisk the oil, vinegar, cinnamon, orange juice, ginger and ginger syrup in a small jug. Season to taste, pour over the salad and toss lightly.

Arrange the reserved figs in pairs over the salad. If you are using the pomegranates, scoop out the seeds, scatter over the salad and serve.

Note: When in season, mandarins and mandarin juice are a delicious alternative to the oranges and orange juice in this salad.

Serves 4

radicchio with figs and ginger vinaigrette

An intensely fresh blast of sharp, savoury salsa swathes tender squid and crisp greens in a snappy embrace.

squid salad with salsa verde

800 g (1 lb 12 oz) smallish
  squid, cleaned, scored
  and sliced into 4 cm
  (1¹/₂ inch) diamonds
2 tbs olive oil
2 tbs lime juice
150 g (5¹/₂ oz) green beans,
  trimmed and halved
175 g (6 oz) snowpeas
  (mangetout), tailed
100 g (3¹/₂ oz) baby rocket
  (arugula) leaves

salsa verde
1 thick slice white bread,
  crusts removed
140 ml (5 fl oz) olive oil
3 tbs finely chopped parsley
2 tsp finely grated lemon zest
3 tbs lemon juice
2 anchovy fillets, finely chopped
2 tbs capers, rinsed and drained
1 garlic clove, crushed

Toss the squid in a bowl with the oil, lime juice and a little salt and pepper. Cover with plastic wrap, refrigerate and leave to marinate for 2 hours.

To make the salsa verde, break the bread into chunks and drizzle with 2 tablespoons of the oil, mixing it in with your hands so it is absorbed. Place the bread and remaining oil in a food processor with the remaining salsa verde ingredients, and blend to a paste. If the mixture is too thick, thin it with a little extra lemon juice and olive oil, to taste.

Bring a pot of lightly salted water to the boil, add the beans and blanch until just tender, about 2–3 minutes. Remove with tongs, refresh under cold water, then drain well. Blanch the snowpeas in the same pot for 1 minute, then drain, refresh in cold water and drain again.

Meanwhile, preheat a barbecue grill or chargrill pan (griddle) to high. Cook the squid in batches for 3 minutes per batch, or until cooked. Take off the heat, allow to cool slightly and toss in a bowl with the beans, snowpeas and rocket. Add 3 tablespoons of salsa verde and toss gently. Arrange on a serving platter, drizzle with the remaining salsa verde and serve.

Serves 4

squid salad with salsa verde

moroccan lamb salad

spice mix
2 garlic cloves, crushed
1 tsp ground cumin
1 tsp harissa (see Note)
1 tsp ground coriander

125 ml (4 fl oz/^{1}/$_2$ cup) olive oil
2 large handfuls coriander,
   finely chopped
2 tbs lemon juice
3 tbs chopped parsley
^{1}/$_2$ tsp ground turmeric
2 lamb backstraps or loin fillets
   (600 g/1 lb 5 oz), trimmed
250 g (9 oz/1 cup) thick plain
   yoghurt

50 g (1^3/$_4$ oz) baby rocket
   (arugula) leaves

pistachio couscous
125 ml (4 fl oz/^{1}/$_2$ cup)
   orange juice
2 tbs lemon juice
^{1}/$_2$ tsp ground cinnamon
250 g (9 oz/1^1/$_3$ cups) instant
   couscous
50 g (1^3/$_4$ oz) butter
35 g (1^1/$_4$ oz/^{1}/$_4$ cup) currants
50 g (1^3/$_4$ oz/heaped ^{1}/$_3$ cup)
   chopped pistachio nuts
425 g (15 oz) tin chickpeas,
   rinsed and drained
3 tbs chopped parsley

In a small bowl, combine the spice mix ingredients. Put the oil in a large, non-metallic bowl and stir in half the spice mix and all the coriander, lemon juice, parsley and turmeric. Mix well. Add the lamb, turning to coat well. Cover with plastic wrap and refrigerate for 1 hour.

Mix the remaining spice mix together with the yoghurt, then cover and refrigerate until needed.

To make the pistachio couscous, pour the orange juice and lemon juice into a measuring jug, then add enough water to make 300 ml (10^1/$_2$ fl oz). Pour into a saucepan, add the cinnamon and bring to the boil. Remove from the heat, pour in the couscous, cover and leave for 5 minutes. Add the butter and fluff up the couscous with a fork, raking out any lumps, then fold in the currants, pistachios, chickpeas and parsley.

Meanwhile, preheat a barbecue grill or chargrill pan (griddle) to high. Drain the marinade from the lamb and cook for 2 minutes on each side, or until charred on the outside but still pink in the middle. Remove from the heat, cover with foil and rest for 5 minutes, then slice across the grain.

45

Divide the couscous between four large serving plates and top with the rocket and lamb slices. Top with a dollop of the yoghurt mixture and serve.

Note: Harissa is a fiery Middle Eastern chilli paste readily available from delicatessens or specialist food stores.

Serves 4

moroccan lamb salad

three-bean salad

100 g (3^1/$_2$ oz) green beans, trimmed and cut into 4 cm (1^1/$_2$ inch) lengths
200 g (7 oz) frozen broad (fava) beans, defrosted
310 g (10^1/$_2$ oz) tin butter beans, rinsed and drained
310 g (10^1/$_2$ oz) tin red kidney beans, rinsed and drained
1 small red onion, finely sliced
2 tbs chopped parsley
2 tbs ready-made French dressing

Bring a small pot of lightly salted water to the boil. Add the green beans and broad beans. Stand for 1 minute over the heat, then drain. Refresh under cold water, then drain again.

Place the green beans and broad beans in a serving bowl with all the tinned beans, onion and parsley. Pour the dressing over and toss well.

Serves 4 as a side salad

roasted tomato and pasta salad with pesto

140 ml (5 fl oz) olive oil
500 g (1 lb 2 oz/2 punnets)
   cherry tomatoes
5 garlic cloves, unpeeled
400 g (14 oz) orecchiette or
   other shell-shaped pasta

90 g (3¼ oz/⅓ cup)
   ready-made pesto
3 tbs balsamic vinegar
basil leaves, to serve

Preheat the oven to 180°C (350°F/Gas 4). Put 2 tablespoons of the oil in a roasting tin and leave to warm in the hot oven for 5 minutes. Add the cherry tomatoes and garlic, season well and toss until the tomatoes are well coated. Return to the oven and roast for 20 minutes (be sure to keep all the pan juices for the dressing).

Meanwhile, cook the pasta in a large pot of rapidly boiling salted water until al dente. Drain well and transfer to a large serving bowl.

Squeeze the flesh from the roasted garlic cloves into a bowl. Add the remaining oil, pesto, vinegar and 3 tablespoons of the pan juices from the roasted tomatoes. Season with a little salt and pepper, then toss to combine. Add to the pasta and mix well to coat. Gently stir in the roasted tomatoes, then scatter with basil leaves. Serve warm or cold.

Serves 4

roasted tomato and pasta salad with pesto

The humble chicken hits fresh new heights when given a smart dressing down by a piquant salsa verde.

chicken with green chilli salsa verde

green chilli salsa verde
1 green capsicum (pepper), roughly chopped
1–2 long green chillies, seeded and chopped
1 garlic clove, chopped
1 handful flat-leaf (Italian) parsley
1 handful basil
3 spring onions (scallions), finely chopped
1 tbs lemon juice
1 tbs olive oil

4 chicken breast fillets (about 200 g/7 oz each)
70 g (2^{1}/$_{2}$ oz/2^{1}/$_{3}$ cups) watercress sprigs
3 celery stalks, sliced

To make the salsa verde, put the capsicum, chilli, garlic, parsley and basil in a food processor and blend to a purée. Transfer the mixture to a sieve and leave to sit for 20 minutes to drain, then transfer to a bowl and stir in the spring onion, lemon juice and oil. Season with salt and pepper.

Meanwhile, preheat a barbecue grill or chargrill pan (griddle) to medium. Add the chicken and cook for 6–8 minutes on one side. Turn and cook for a further 5 minutes, or until cooked through — the exact cooking time will vary depending on the heat of your barbecue and the thickness of your chicken fillets. Leave to cool slightly, then shred into a large bowl.

While the chicken is still warm, add the salsa verde and toss to coat well. Combine the watercress and celery in a serving dish, top with the chicken and salsa verde mixture, toss gently and serve at once.

Serves 4

53

chicken with green chilli salsa verde

Sweet, juicy mango is the perfect partner to soft, flaky salmon and together they're pretty as a picture — a symphony in pink.

seared asian salmon salad

700 g (1 lb 9 oz) salmon fillets
1 tbs olive oil
2 tbs lime juice
1 tbs soy sauce
2 tbs runny honey
2 ripe mangoes, peeled and
   thinly sliced
200 g (7 oz) bean sprouts,
   tails trimmed
1 small cos (romaine) lettuce,
   leaves separated

1 handful coriander (cilantro)
   leaves

asian dressing
1 tbs olive oil
1 tbs fish sauce
2 tbs lime juice
1 small red chilli, finely chopped
1/2 tsp sugar

Remove any pin bones from the salmon and put the fillets in a single layer in a shallow non-metallic dish. In a small bowl, whisk the oil, lime juice, soy sauce and honey. Pour the mixture over the salmon, ensuring it coats all sides of the fish. Cover and refrigerate for 30 minutes.

Meanwhile, put all the Asian dressing ingredients in a small bowl and whisk until well combined. Set aside until needed.

Preheat a barbecue grill or chargrill pan (griddle) to high. If you like your salmon slightly pink in the middle, cook the fillets for 5 minutes on one side, then turn and cook the second side for a further 4 minutes. If you prefer it cooked all the way through, leave it for an extra minute on the second side. The exact cooking time will vary depending on the heat of your barbecue and the thickness of your salmon fillets. Leave the salmon to cool slightly, then break into chunks.

Put the mango, bean sprouts and lettuce leaves in a serving bowl, add the salmon chunks and toss gently. Pour over the dressing, scatter with the coriander and serve at once.

Note: Add the dressing just before serving so the bean sprouts and lettuce leaves don't become soggy.

Serves 4

seared asian salmon salad

Olives and capers fire intense bursts of flavour into seductively salty haloumi, hosed down by cooling cubes of cucumber.

grilled haloumi salad with herb dressing

1 large Lebanese (short) cucumber, seeded and diced
3 tomatoes, seeded and diced
40 g (1$\frac{1}{2}$ oz/$\frac{1}{4}$ cup) pitted and halved Kalamata olives
2 tbs capers, rinsed and drained
1 small red onion, finely diced
300 g (10$\frac{1}{2}$ oz) haloumi cheese, cut into 1 cm ($\frac{1}{2}$ inch) slices

herb dressing
1 garlic clove, roughly chopped
1 small handful basil leaves
1 small handful flat-leaf (Italian) parsley
3 tbs olive oil
2 tbs lemon juice

Heat a barbecue grill or chargrill pan (griddle) to medium. While it is heating, prepare the salad: simply put the cucumber, tomato, olives, capers and onion in a serving dish and mix together gently.

To make the herb dressing, crush the garlic in a mortar and pestle with a pinch of salt. Add the basil and parsley and pound until a paste starts to form. Add a little of the oil and pound for another 10 seconds. Stir in the remaining oil and lemon juice and season with black pepper. (If you prefer, purée the ingredients in a food processor.) Set aside.

Chargrill the haloumi for about 1–2 minutes on each side, or until it is starting to soften but not melt. Cut the haloumi into thick strips and arrange on top of the salad. Spoon the dressing over the top and serve at once while the haloumi is still hot, before it becomes rubbery and tough.

Serves 4

grilled haloumi salad with herb dressing

ladies who lunch   Lingering over an elegant lunch with the ladies who matter the most to you can be a wicked and gossipy delight. Keep it fresh and keep it light, as a virtuous lunch leaves

plenty of room for one more glass of white. Girly lunches are not just a luxury, but an essential element of a civilized way of life — a joyful celebration of female friendship.

Banish any notion of ladies who lunch as idle creatures with too much time and money and not enough to do. Lunching with your girlfriends is one of life's most sublime pleasures and a luxury available to all of us — an exploration of lives, loves and longings. Even if your mates are a gaggle of goodtime girls, the chances are most of you will be watching your waistline. If there's a time to count kilojoules, carbohydrates and fat of all kinds this is it, so keep this chapter close at hand. All the recipes assembled within it are either low carb or low fat, specifically suited to the diet-conscious eater. You can enjoy these luscious salads to your heart's content, without sacrificing good taste on the altar of shapeliness. Plating it up is another delicious aspect of putting on a girly lunch — if you've ever yearned to indulge your inner child, the one who secretly longs for something pretty in pink, this is the time to cut loose. Florals, pinks and pretty napkins don't have to be fusty and faded, nor should delicate china be relegated to the back of the cupboard. Pull it all out and funk it up with a shot of intense colour or search around for a pearly pink made fresh with a modish pattern. Whether you lean towards Jane Austen or Marilyn Monroe there are myriad ways to make it pretty but keep it modern. Sacrifice is not a notion that should play a part in any celebration, even an everyday one. Moderation can be the enemy of variety and flavour, but you can make it moreish without being bad. Serve up salads and your girlfriends will thank you when they indulge in that extra glass.

scallop, ginger and spinach salad

300 g (10¹/₂ oz) scallops,
    without roe
oil, for brushing
100 g (3¹/₂ oz) baby English
    spinach leaves
1 small red capsicum (pepper),
    very finely julienned
50 g (1³/₄ oz/heaped ¹/₂ cup)
    bean sprouts, tails trimmed

sake dressing
25 ml (1 fl oz) sake
1 tbs lime juice
2 tsp shaved palm sugar or
    soft brown sugar
1 tsp fish sauce

Slice or pull off any vein, membrane or hard white muscle from the scallops. Rinse the scallops and pat dry with paper towels. Put all the sake dressing ingredients in a small bowl and mix until the sugar has dissolved.

Heat a chargrill pan (griddle) or barbecue hotplate to high and lightly brush with oil. Cook the scallops in batches for 1 minute on each side, or until just cooked.

Divide the spinach, capsicum and bean sprouts between four plates. Arrange the scallops on top, pour over the dressing and serve at once.

Serves 4

vietnamese prawn salad

1/2 Chinese cabbage
1/2 red onion, finely sliced
500 g (1 lb 2 oz) cooked tiger
    prawns (shrimp), peeled
    and deveined, tails intact
1 handful coriander (cilantro)
    leaves, chopped
1 handful Vietnamese mint
    leaves, chopped

whole Vietnamese mint leaves,
    to serve

dressing
2 tbs sugar
2 tbs fish sauce
3 tbs lime juice
1 tbs white vinegar

Shred the cabbage finely and place in a large bowl. Cover with plastic wrap and chill for 30 minutes.

Just before serving, put all the dressing ingredients in a small jug with 1/2 teaspoon salt and mix well to dissolve the sugar.

In a serving bowl, toss together the shredded cabbage, onion, prawns, coriander and mint. Pour over the dressing, toss through gently, garnish with a few whole mint leaves and serve.

Serves 4

scallop, ginger and spinach salad

roast duck salad with chilli dressing

chilli dressing
1/2 tsp chilli flakes
2 1/2 tbs fish sauce
1 tbs lime juice
2 tsp grated palm sugar or
    soft brown sugar

1 Chinese roasted duck
1 small red onion, thinly sliced
1 tbs julienned fresh ginger
4 tbs roughly chopped coriander
   (cilantro)
4 tbs roughly chopped mint
80 g (1/2 cup) roasted unsalted
    cashew nuts
8 butter lettuce leaves

To make the chilli dressing, put the chilli flakes in a frying pan and dry-fry over medium heat for 30 seconds, then grind to a powder in a mortar and pestle or spice grinder. Put the powder in a small bowl with the fish sauce, lime juice and sugar; mix well to dissolve the sugar and set aside.

Remove the flesh from the duck, cut it into bite-sized pieces and put it in a bowl. Add the onion, ginger, coriander, mint and cashews. Pour in the dressing and toss together gently.

Arrange the lettuce on a serving platter, or use the leaves to line individual serving bowls. Top with the duck salad and serve.

Serves 4

prawn and fennel salad

1.25 kg (2 lb 12 oz) raw large
    prawns (shrimp), peeled
    and deveined
1 large fennel bulb (about
    400 g/14 oz), thinly sliced
300 g (10$^{1/2}$ oz/$^{1/2}$ large bunch)
    watercress, picked
2 tbs finely snipped chives

lemon and dijon dressing
3 tbs lemon juice
125 ml (4 fl oz/$^{1/2}$ cup)
    extra virgin olive oil
1 tbs Dijon mustard
1 large garlic clove, finely
    chopped

Bring a large pot of water to the boil. Add the prawns, return to the boil and simmer for 2 minutes, or until the prawns turn pink and are cooked through. Drain and leave to cool. Pat the prawns dry with paper towels, slice them in half lengthways and put in a large serving bowl. Add the fennel, watercress and chives and mix well.

Whisk all the lemon and Dijon dressing ingredients together in a small bowl until well combined. Pour the dressing over the salad, season with salt and cracked black pepper and toss gently. Arrange the salad on four serving plates and serve at once.

Serves 4

roast duck salad with chilli dressing

The sting of sweet heat, tender beef and fresh, zesty salad blow out the senses but not the waistline.

thai beef salad

600 g (1 lb 5 oz) beef fillet, trimmed
2 tbs fish sauce
1 tbs peanut oil
2 vine-ripened tomatoes, each cut into 8 wedges
1/2 butter lettuce, leaves separated

mint and chilli dressing
1 small dried red chilli, roughly chopped
4 tbs fish sauce
4 red Asian shallots, finely sliced
2 spring onions (scallions), thinly sliced on the diagonal
4 tbs mint leaves
4 tbs coriander (cilantro) leaves
1 garlic clove, crushed
100 ml (3 1/2 fl oz) lime juice
2 tsp grated palm sugar or soft brown sugar

Put the beef in a bowl and pour over the fish sauce. Cover and refrigerate for 3 hours, turning the meat several times to coat.

Put a baking tray in the oven and preheat the oven to 220°C (425°F/Gas 7). Heat the oil in a frying pan and cook the beef fillet over high heat for 1 minute on each side, or until browned, then place on the hot baking tray and roast for 15 minutes for a medium-rare result. Remove from the oven, cover loosely with foil and allow to rest for 10 minutes.

Meanwhile, make the mint and chilli dressing. Put a small, non-stick frying pan over medium–high heat. Add the chilli and dry-fry for 1–2 minutes, or until dark but not burnt. Transfer to a mortar and pestle or spice mill and grind to a fine powder. Place in a bowl with the remaining dressing ingredients, stirring to dissolve the sugar.

Thinly slice the beef and toss in a bowl with the dressing and tomato. Arrange the lettuce on a serving platter and pile the beef salad on top. Serve warm.

Serves 4

thai beef salad

crab salad with green mango and coconut

dressing
2 garlic cloves, peeled
1 small red chilli
1¹/2 tbs dried shrimp
1¹/2 tbs fish sauce
2 tbs lime juice
2 tsp palm sugar or soft
   brown sugar

4 tbs shredded coconut
   (see Note)
200 g (7 oz/2 cups) shredded
   green mango (see Note)
1 small handful mint leaves
   (torn if very big)

1 small handful coriander
   (cilantro) leaves
2 kaffir (makrut) lime leaves,
   shredded
1¹/2 tsp thinly shredded pickled
   ginger
350 g (12 oz) fresh crab meat
4 small squares banana leaves
   (optional)
50 g (1³/4 oz/¹/3 cup) chopped
   toasted unsalted peanuts
4 lime wedges

Preheat the oven to 180°C (350°F/Gas 4). To make the dressing, pound the garlic, chilli, dried shrimp and ¹/2 teaspoon salt to a paste in a mortar and pestle. Whisk in the fish sauce, lime juice and sugar with a fork.

Spread the shredded coconut on a baking tray and bake for 1–2 minutes, shaking the tray occasionally to ensure even toasting. Watch the coconut closely, as it will burn easily.

Put the shredded mango in a large bowl and add the mint, coriander, lime leaves, ginger, coconut and crab meat. Pour the dressing over the top and toss together gently.

If using the banana leaves, place a square in each serving bowl (the leaves are for presentation only and are not edible). Mound some crab salad on top, sprinkle with the peanuts and serve immediately with lime wedges.

Note: Freshly shredded coconut is delicious, so if you have the time, remove the skin from a coconut and shred the flesh using a vegetable peeler. For this recipe you will need about 3 green mangoes to get the right quantity of shredded mango flesh.

Serves 4

crab salad with green mango and coconut

chargrilled tomato salad

8 Roma (plum) tomatoes
1$\frac{1}{2}$ tsp capers, rinsed and drained
4 basil leaves, torn
3 tsp olive oil
3 tsp balsamic vinegar
1 garlic clove, crushed
$\frac{1}{4}$ tsp honey

Cut the tomatoes lengthways into quarters and scoop out the seeds. Heat a chargrill pan (griddle) to medium and cook the tomato quarters for 1–2 minutes on each side, or until grill marks appear and the tomatoes have softened. Cool to room temperature and place in a bowl.

Combine the capers, basil, oil, vinegar, garlic and honey in a small bowl and season with salt and freshly ground black pepper. Pour the mixture over the tomatoes and toss together gently. Serve at room temperature with crusty bread and grilled meats.

Serves 4 as a side salad

south-western black bean salad

165 g (5³/4 oz/³/4 cup) dried
   black (turtle) beans
150 g (5¹/2 oz/³/4 cup) dried
   cannellini beans
1 small red onion, chopped
1 small red capsicum (pepper),
   chopped
265 g (9¹/2 oz/1¹/3 cups) tinned
   corn kernels, drained

3 tbs chopped coriander
   (cilantro)

dressing
1 garlic clove, crushed
¹/2 tsp ground cumin
¹/2 tsp French mustard
2 tbs red wine vinegar
3 tbs olive oil

Put the black beans and cannellini beans in separate bowls, cover with plenty of cold water and leave to soak overnight. Rinse well, then drain and place in separate pots and cover with water. Bring both pots of water to the boil, reduce the heat and simmer for 45 minutes, or until the beans are tender. Drain, rinse and allow to cool, then put all the beans in a serving bowl. Mix through the onion, capsicum, corn and coriander.

To make the dressing, combine the garlic, cumin, mustard and vinegar in a small jug, then gradually whisk in the oil. Season lightly with salt and pepper. Pour over the bean mixture, toss lightly to combine and serve.

Serves 4 as a side salad

chargrilled tomato salad

smoked trout with chilli raspberry dressing

160 g (5³/4 oz/2 bunches) sorrel
1 small smoked trout
12 asparagus spears, trimmed
1 small red onion, thinly sliced
200 g (7 oz) pear tomatoes,
   halved
150 g (5¹/2 oz/1 punnet)
   raspberries

chilli raspberry dressing
100 g (3¹/2 oz/²/3 punnet)
   raspberries
¹/2 tsp chilli paste
1 garlic clove, crushed
4 tbs olive oil
1¹/2 tbs raspberry vinegar
   or white wine vinegar

Trim the stalks from the sorrel, rinse the leaves well, pat them dry and put in the refrigerator to crisp. Peel away and discard the skin and bones from the trout. Break the flesh into pieces.

Put the chilli raspberry dressing ingredients in a small pan over low heat until the raspberries begin to break up and colour the liquid. Transfer to a bowl, whisk well and season with salt and freshly ground black pepper.

Boil, steam or microwave the asparagus until just tender, then drain and refresh under cold water. Drain again. Divide the sorrel between individual plates. Arrange the asparagus, trout, onion, tomatoes and raspberries on top, drizzle with the dressing and serve.

Serves 4

roast cherry tomato and chicken salad

250 g (9 oz/1 punnet) cherry
    tomatoes or small truss
    tomatoes
2 whole garlic cloves, unpeeled
1 tbs olive oil
1 thyme sprig, cut into 3 pieces

1 barbecued chicken
100 g (3¹/2 oz) baby rocket
    (arugula) leaves
2 tbs capers, rinsed and drained
    (optional)
1 tbs balsamic vinegar

Preheat the oven to 180°C (350°F/Gas 4). Put the tomatoes, whole garlic cloves, oil and thyme in a roasting tin and bake for 15 minutes.

Meanwhile, remove the meat from the chicken, discarding the skin and bones. Shred the meat and toss in a bowl with the rocket and capers.

Allow the cooked tomatoes to cool slightly, then gently squash each one to release some of the juice. Add the tomatoes to the chicken mixture, leaving the garlic and pan juices in the roasting dish. Discard the thyme. Squeeze the flesh from each roasted garlic clove and mix with any pan juices. Add the vinegar and mix again. Pour the mixture over the salad, toss gently and serve.

Serves 4

roast cherry tomato and chicken salad

thai noodle salad

250 g (9 oz) dried instant
    egg noodles
500 g (1 lb 2 oz) cooked large
    prawns (shrimp), peeled
    and deveined, tails intact
5 spring onions (scallions), sliced
2 tbs chopped coriander
    (cilantro)
1 red capsicum (pepper), diced
100 g (3 1/2 oz) snowpeas
    (mangetout), julienned
4 lime wedges

dressing
2 tbs grated fresh ginger
2 tbs soy sauce
2 tbs sesame oil
4 tbs red wine vinegar
1 tbs sweet chilli sauce
2 garlic cloves, crushed
4 tbs kecap manis

Cook the egg noodles in a pot of boiling water for 2 minutes, or until tender. Drain thoroughly, then leave to cool in a large serving bowl.

Whisk all the dressing ingredients together in a bowl and gently mix through the cooled noodles. Add the prawns, spring onion, coriander, capsicum and snowpeas. Toss gently and serve with lime wedges.

Serves 4

marinated fish salad with chilli and basil

500 g (1 lb 2 oz) skinless firm
   white fish fillets
3 tbs lime juice
3 tbs light coconut milk
mixed salad leaves, to serve
3 tomatoes, diced
3 Lebanese (short) cucumbers,
   diced

5 spring onions (scallions),
   finely sliced
2 red chillies, seeded and sliced
2 garlic cloves, crushed
1 tsp grated fresh ginger
1 large handful basil leaves,
   chopped

Slice the fish into thin strips and place in a non-metallic bowl. Put the lime juice and coconut milk in a jug with 1 teaspoon salt and $1/4$ teaspoon of cracked black pepper. Mix well, then pour over the fish. Cover and refrigerate for several hours or overnight, turning once or twice. (The acid in the lime juice will 'cook' the fish, firming the flesh and turning it opaque.)

Arrange some salad leaves on four serving plates. Gently mix the tomato, cucumber, spring onion, chilli, garlic and ginger through the fish, spoon over the salad leaves and serve.

Note: When mangoes are in season, peel and roughly dice the flesh and toss it through the finished salad for extra flavour and sweetness.

Serves 4

thai noodle salad

garden salad

1/2 green oakleaf lettuce
150 g (51/2 oz/1 bunch) rocket
 (arugula), trimmed
1 small radicchio lettuce
1 green capsicum (pepper),
 cut into thin strips
zest of 1 lemon

dressing
1 tbs roughly chopped coriander
 (cilantro)
11/2 tbs lemon juice
1 tsp soft brown sugar
1 tbs olive oil
1 garlic clove, crushed (optional)

Wash and dry the salad greens thoroughly, then tear into bite-sized pieces. Toss in a large serving bowl with the capsicum and lemon zest.

Whisk the dressing ingredients in a small mixing bowl until the sugar has dissolved. Just before serving, pour the dressing over the salad and toss well.

Serves 4 as a side salad

borlotti bean, beetroot and mint salad

400 g (14 oz) tin borlotti beans,
   drained and rinsed (see Note)
450 g (1 lb) tin baby beetroot,
   drained and chopped
150 g (5^1/$_2$ oz) cherry tomatoes,
   halved
1 handful mint leaves

dressing
1 tbs apple cider vinegar or
   white wine vinegar
1 tbs olive oil

Put the beans, beetroot and cherry tomatoes in a serving dish. Roughly chop half the mint leaves and mix them through the salad. Whisk the dressing ingredients in a small bowl and season to taste. Pour over the salad and mix gently. Scatter over the remaining mint leaves and serve.

Note: When available, use fresh borlotti beans in this recipe. First blanch them in a pot of boiling water for several minutes until tender.

Serves 4 as a side salad

borlotti bean, beetroot and mint salad

Tender young spring vegetables are a gift of nature and are at their best in this delicate salad with its zesty dressing.

chicken and spring vegetable salad

600 g (1 lb 5 oz) chicken breast
    fillets
1/2 lime, juiced
4 kaffir (makrut) lime leaves,
    shredded
1/2 onion, peeled
6 black peppercorns
175 g (6 oz/1 bunch) asparagus

175 g (6 oz/1 1/4 cups) broad (fava)
    beans, defrosted if frozen
225 g (8 oz) baby green beans

lemon tarragon dressing
1 tbs olive oil
2 tbs lemon juice
2 tbs chopped tarragon leaves

Half-fill a large pot with water. Add the chicken, lime juice, lime leaves, onion and peppercorns. Cover and bring slowly to the boil, then reduce the heat and simmer for 3 minutes. Turn off the heat and leave the chicken to cool in the broth for at least 30 minutes — it will continue to cook during this time.

Meanwhile, combine the lemon tarragon dressing ingredients in a small bowl. Season lightly with salt and pepper, mix well and set aside.

Snap the woody ends off the asparagus and discard. Bring another pot of water to the boil and add a pinch of salt. Add the broad beans and cook for 1 minute, then add the green beans and simmer for 1 minute. Now add the asparagus and cook for another minute. Drain well and refresh under cold water. Drain well again.

Slice the asparagus spears lengthways and place them in a serving dish with the green beans. Remove the skins from the broad beans and add the beans to the serving dish.

Remove the cooled chicken from the poaching liquid. Shred the fillets, then gently toss them through the salad with the dressing. Serve at once.

Serves 4

chicken and spring vegetable salad

snowpea salad with japanese dressing

200 g (7 oz) snowpeas
    (mangetout), tailed
50 g (1³/4 oz/¹/2 punnet)
    snowpea (mangetout)
    sprouts
1 small red capsicum (pepper),
    julienned
2 tsp toasted sesame seeds

japanese dressing
¹/2 tsp dashi granules
1 tbs soy sauce
1 tbs mirin
1 tsp soft brown sugar
1 garlic clove, crushed
1 tsp finely chopped fresh ginger
¹/4 tsp sesame oil
1 tbs vegetable oil
2 tsp toasted sesame seeds

Bring a pot of water to the boil, add the snowpeas and blanch for 1 minute. Drain and refresh under cold water, then drain again. Toss in a serving bowl with the snowpea sprouts and capsicum.

To make the dressing, dissolve the dashi granules in 1¹/2 tablespoons of hot water. Pour into a small bowl, add the remaining dressing ingredients and whisk well. Pour the dressing over the snowpeas, toss well and season to taste. Sprinkle with the sesame seeds and serve.

Serves 4 as a side salad

pear and sprout salad with sesame dressing

2 small firm, ripe pears
200 g (7 oz/2 punnets) snowpea
   (mangetout) sprouts
200 g (7 oz) bean sprouts,
   tails trimmed
1 small bunch chives, snipped
   into 4 cm (1½ inch) lengths
65 g (2¼ oz) snowpeas
   (mangetout), julienned
1 celery stalk, julienned

1 small handful coriander
   (cilantro) sprigs
1 tsp sesame seeds

sesame dressing
1½ tbs soy sauce
1 tsp sesame oil
3 tsp soft brown sugar
1½ tbs peanut oil
3 tsp rice vinegar

Peel and core the pears, then slice them into thin strips. Put the pear strips in a bowl and cover with water to prevent discolouration.

Put all the sesame dressing ingredients in a small screw-top jar and shake well to dissolve the sugar.

Drain the pears and put in a large serving bowl with the snowpea sprouts, bean sprouts, chives, snowpeas, celery and coriander. Pour the dressing over, toss lightly, sprinkle with the sesame seeds and serve.

Serves 4 as a side salad

snowpea salad with japanese dressing

lunchbox Hasty lunches snatched from the work canteen are the downfall of many a dedicated dieter, health nut or office gourmand, and yet organizing a packed lunch can seem all too daunting in the cold light of morning. Not anymore. Here's all the inspiration you need to plan ahead a little and pack a pretty lunchbox with a super energy-giving salad to power you through the day.

Being aware of what we eat is not just about watching our weight. For many of us it is simply about aspiring to an optimal state of health and wellbeing. Evaluating the quality of the food we consume is a simple way to stay on top and, by and large, most of us manage to do pretty well, except for the daily downfall — lunch on the run. If you're in the habit of buying lunch, whether from a food court, deli, canteen or fast-food joint, it can be hard to know what you are really consuming. And while schooldays may have ruined your appetite for packed lunches, it's time to relinquish those musty memories of soggy sandwiches and browning bananas. Variety, sustenance and balance are easy to achieve on a daily basis when you explore the range of delicious salads that are perfect for packing up and taking with you. It's so simple to create inspiring and healthy lunches: all the recipes in this chapter can be made ahead and packed the night before, ready to pop in your bag as you're dashing out the door. Even better, there's enough for two helpings, so pack another lunchbox for a loved one, or save it for the following day. And when it comes to stashing your salad, you can always resort to the ever-sensible plastic lunchbox, or you could really have some fun and break up the humdrum routine. Noodle boxes, kitsch creations and tiffin stacks are just a couple of ideas to dress it all up. Takeaway chopsticks and funky napkins are a cute way to treat yourself as you would someone else — like you are special and deserve the extra treatment. Now there's something to look forward to in the middle of the workaday day!

asian tofu salad

1/2 red capsicum (pepper)
1/2 green capsicum (pepper)
60 g (2 1/4 oz/2/3 cup) bean
   sprouts, tails trimmed
2 spring onions (scallions), sliced
1 tbs chopped coriander (cilantro)
200 g (7 oz/3 cups) shredded
   Chinese cabbage
1 1/2 tbs chopped roasted peanuts
200 g (7 oz) firm tofu
1 1/2 tbs peanut oil

dressing

1 tbs sweet chilli sauce
1 tbs lime juice
1/4 tsp sesame oil
3 tsp light soy sauce
1 garlic clove, finely chopped
1 1/2 tsp finely grated fresh
   ginger
1 1/2 tbs peanut oil

Thinly slice the red and green capsicum and toss in a large bowl with the bean sprouts, spring onion, coriander, cabbage and peanuts.

Cut the tofu into 8 x 2 cm (3 1/4 x 3/4 inch) steaks. Heat the oil in a large frying pan and cook the tofu over medium heat for 2–3 minutes on each side, or until golden with a crispy edge. Add the tofu to the salad.

To make the dressing, whisk all the ingredients in a small bowl until well combined. Toss through the salad and divide between two lunchboxes.

Makes 2 lunchbox salads

asian pork salad

ginger and chilli dressing
3 cm (1¼ inch) piece of fresh
   ginger, peeled and julienned
1 tsp rice vinegar
½ small red chilli, seeded
   and finely chopped
1 tbs light soy sauce
a few drops of sesame oil
½ star anise
1 tsp lime juice

125 g (4½ oz) Chinese roast
   pork (char siu)
50 g (1¾ oz/½ punnet)
   snowpea (mangetout)
   sprouts
2 spring onions (scallions), thinly
   sliced on the diagonal
½ small red capsicum (pepper),
   thinly sliced

To make the ginger and chilli dressing, combine the ginger, vinegar, chilli, soy sauce, sesame oil, star anise and lime juice in a small saucepan. Gently warm for 2 minutes, or until just about to come to the boil, then set aside to cool. Once it has cooled, remove the star anise.

Thinly slice the pork and divide among two lunchboxes along with the snowpea sprouts, spring onion and capsicum. Pack the dressing separately and drizzle over the salad just before eating.

Makes 2 lunchbox salads

asian pork salad

farfalle salad with sun-dried tomatoes and spinach

165 g (5³/4 oz) farfalle or
   spiral pasta
1 spring onion (scallion), finely
   sliced on the diagonal
3 sun-dried tomatoes, cut
   into strips
350 g (12 oz) English spinach,
   stalks trimmed and leaves
   shredded

1 tbs toasted pine nuts
1 tsp chopped oregano

dressing
1 tbs olive oil
¹/4 tsp chopped chilli
1 small garlic clove, crushed

116

Cook the pasta in a large pot of rapidly boiling salted water until al dente. Drain, rinse under cold water and drain again. Allow the pasta to cool, then transfer to a large bowl. Add the spring onion, tomato, spinach, pine nuts and oregano.

Put all the dressing ingredients in a small screw-top jar and season with salt and pepper. Shake well and pour all over the salad. Gently toss together and divide between two lunchboxes.

Makes 2 lunchbox salads

haloumi and asparagus salad with salsa verde

salsa verde
1 small handful basil leaves
1 small handful mint leaves
1 large handful parsley leaves
1 tbs baby capers, rinsed
   and drained
1 garlic clove
1 tbs olive oil

1/2 tbs lemon juice
1/2 tbs lime juice

125 g (41/2 oz) haloumi cheese
175 g (6 oz/1 bunch) thin
   asparagus spears
1 tbs garlic oil or olive oil
50 g (13/4 oz) mixed salad leaves

To make the salsa verde, blend the herbs, capers, garlic and oil in a food processor until smooth. Add the lemon and lime juice, and pulse briefly.

Heat a chargrill pan (griddle) to medium. Cut the haloumi into 1 cm (1/2 inch) slices, then cut each slice into two small triangles. Brush the haloumi and asparagus with the garlic oil. Chargrill the asparagus for 1 minute or until just tender, then chargrill the haloumi for about 45 seconds on each side, or until grill marks appear.

Divide the salad leaves between two lunchboxes and top with the haloumi and asparagus. Pack the salsa verde separately and drizzle over the salad just before eating.

Makes 2 lunchbox salads

haloumi and asparagus salad with salsa verde

avocado, bacon and tomato salad

3 garlic cloves, unpeeled
2 tbs olive oil
3 tsp balsamic vinegar
1 tsp Dijon mustard
125 g (4^1/$_2$ oz) rindless smoked
    back bacon (see Note) or
    middle bacon rashers

50 g (1^3/$_4$ oz) green salad leaves
^{1}/$_2$ small red onion, finely sliced
1 avocado, cut into chunks
2 small firm, ripe tomatoes,
    cut into chunks

Preheat the oven to 180°C (350°F/Gas 4). Place the unpeeled garlic cloves on a baking tray and roast for 30 minutes. Remove, allow to cool, then squeeze the flesh out of the skins and mash in a small bowl. Add the oil, vinegar and mustard, whisk well to make a dressing and season to taste.

Chop the bacon into bite-sized pieces, then cook under a medium-hot grill (broiler) or dry-fry in a frying pan over medium heat for 3–5 minutes, or until crisp. Divide between two lunchboxes with the salad leaves, onion, avocado and tomato. Gently toss together. Pack the dressing separately and, just before eating, give it a good shake and drizzle over the salad.

Note: Smoked back bacon is available from most delicatessens. If you can't obtain any, you can use bacon rashers instead.

Makes 2 lunchbox salads

chilli chicken and cashew salad

2 tsp olive oil
300 g (10^1/$_2$ oz) chicken breast
    fillets
50 g (1^3/$_4$ oz) salad leaves
125 g (4^1/$_2$ oz/^{1}/$_2$ punnet) cherry
    tomatoes, halved
^{1}/$_2$ Lebanese (short) cucumber,
    cut into bite-sized chunks
50 g (1^3/$_4$ oz/^{1}/$_2$ punnet) snowpea
    (mangetout) sprouts, trimmed
40 g (1^1/$_2$ oz/^{1}/$_4$ cup) cashew
    nuts, roughly chopped

dressing
1^1/$_2$ tbs sweet chilli sauce
1 tbs lime juice
1 tsp fish sauce
1 tbs chopped coriander
    (cilantro)
1 small garlic clove, crushed
^{1}/$_2$ small red chilli, finely
    chopped
1 teaspoon grated fresh ginger
2 tsp peanut or sesame oil

Heat the oil in a frying pan or chargrill pan (griddle). Add the chicken and cook over medium heat for 5–8 minutes on each side, or until cooked through. While still hot, slice each breast widthways into strips.

Combine the dressing ingredients in a large bowl and mix well. Toss the warm chicken strips through the dressing and leave to cool slightly. Divide the salad leaves, tomato, cucumber and snowpea sprouts between two lunchboxes and scatter with the cashews. Pack the dressed chicken separately and mix through the salad just before eating.

Makes 2 lunchbox salads

Felix

Max

chilli chicken and cashew salad

tomato and bocconcini salad

basil oil
125 ml (4 fl oz/^{1}/$_2$ cup) olive oil
1 large handful basil leaves,
   torn
1 tbs balsamic vinegar

3 Roma (plum) tomatoes, halved
175 g (6 oz) cherry bocconcini
   or baby mozzarella cheese
80 g (2^3/$_4$ oz) mizuna lettuce
   leaves or baby rocket
   (arugula) leaves

To make the basil oil, put the oil and basil leaves in a saucepan. Stir gently over medium heat for 3–5 minutes, or until very hot but not smoking. Remove from the heat and discard the basil. Reserve 1 tablespoon of the basil oil and mix it with the vinegar; store the remaining basil oil in a clean jar in the refrigerator to use in salad dressings and pasta sauces.

Arrange the tomato, bocconcini and lettuce in two lunchboxes. Drizzle with the basil oil and sprinkle with sea salt and cracked black pepper.

Makes 2 lunchbox salads

caramelized onion and potato salad

1 tbs olive oil
3 red onions, thinly sliced
500 g (1 lb 2 oz) kipfler or new
   potatoes, unpeeled
2 rashers of streaky bacon,
   rind removed
1/2 bunch chives, snipped

lemon mayonnaise
125 g (41/2 oz/ 1/2 cup)
   ready-made whole-egg
   mayonnaise
2 tsp Dijon mustard
1/2 lemon, juiced
1 tbs sour cream

Heat the oil in a large heavy-based frying pan. Add the onion and cook, stirring, over low heat for 40 minutes, or until soft and caramelized.

Cut any large potatoes into large chunks (leave the small ones whole). Cook in boiling water for 10 minutes, or until just tender, then drain. Place in a large bowl with the onion and most of the chives and mix well.

Meanwhile, grill (broil) the bacon rashers until crisp. Drain on crumpled paper towels and allow to cool slightly, then chop coarsely.

Whisk together the lemon mayonnaise ingredients, pour over the salad and toss to coat. Divide between two lunchboxes and sprinkle with the bacon and reserved chives.

Makes 2 lunchbox salads

tomato and bocconcini salad

minty lentil salad

90 g (3¼ oz/½ cup) brown
    lentils
½ chicken or vegetable stock
    cube, crumbled
1 tomato, cut into 1 cm
    (½ inch) cubes
2 spring onions (scallions), sliced

mint dressing
1 tbs oil
1 tsp apple cider vinegar
2 tsp chopped mint
¼ tsp ground cumin
pinch of cayenne pepper

Put the lentils in a pot, cover with cold water and add the stock cube. Bring to the boil, then reduce the heat and simmer for 20 minutes, or until the lentils are tender — don't overcook or the lentils will become mushy. Drain and set aside to cool.

Gently toss the lentils in a bowl with the tomato and spring onion. Put the mint dressing ingredients in a small screw-top jar and shake well. Drizzle the dressing over the salad, toss gently to combine, then divide between two lunchboxes. Delicious with fresh, crusty bread.

Makes 2 lunchbox salads

beetroot and chive salad

12 baby beetroot
2 tablespoons pine nuts or
    pistachio nuts
30 g (1 oz/1 cup) picked
    watercress leaves
1 tbs snipped chives

dressing
$1/4$ tsp honey
$1/4$ tsp Dijon mustard
3 tsp balsamic vinegar
$1^1/2$ tbs olive oil

Preheat the oven to 200°C (400°F/Gas 6). Trim the beetroot bulbs and scrub them well. Put them in a roasting dish, cover with foil and roast for 1 hour, or until tender. Remove from the oven and leave to cool.

Turn the oven down to 180°C (350°F/Gas 4). Spread the nuts on a baking tray and bake for 5 minutes, or until lightly golden, ensuring they don't burn. Remove from the oven, leave to cool, then roughly chop.

To make the dressing, combine the honey, mustard and vinegar in a small jug. Whisk in the oil with a fork until well combined, then season to taste.

Peel the beetroot, wearing gloves, and halve any larger ones. Divide between two lunchboxes with the watercress and chives, and scatter with the nuts. Pack the dressing separately and drizzle over the salad just before eating.

Makes 2 lunchbox salads

beetroot and chive salad

vietnamese salad with lemon grass dressing

100 g (3¹/₂ oz) dried rice
   vermicelli
1 small handful Vietnamese
   mint leaves, torn
1 small handful coriander
   (cilantro) leaves
¹/₂ small red onion, thinly sliced
1 small green mango, peeled
   and julienned
¹/₂ Lebanese (short) cucumber,
   halved and thinly sliced
80 g (2³/₄ oz/¹/₂ cup) crushed
   peanuts

lemon grass dressing

3 tbs lime juice
2 tsp grated palm sugar or
   soft brown sugar
1¹/₂ tbs seasoned rice vinegar
1 stem lemon grass, white part
   only, finely chopped
1 red chilli, seeded and finely
   chopped
1 makrut (kaffir lime) leaf,
   shredded

Put the noodles in a bowl, cover with boiling water and soak for 10 minutes, or until soft. Drain, rinse under cold water and cut into short lengths. Toss in a large bowl with the mint, coriander, onion, mango, cucumber and three-quarters of the nuts, then divide between two lunchboxes.

Whisk the dressing ingredients together and toss through the salad. Pack the remaining nuts separately and sprinkle over the salad just before eating.

Makes 2 lunchbox salads

cottage cheese salad

1/2 sheet lavash bread
1 tsp canola oil
pinch of mild paprika
1 tbs snipped chives
250 g (9 oz) cottage cheese

8 red oakleaf lettuce leaves
100 g (3 1/2 oz) red grapes
1 small carrot, grated
2 tbs alfalfa sprouts

Preheat the oven to 180°C (350°F/Gas 4). Brush the lavash with the oil, sprinkle lightly with paprika and cut into eight strips. Spread on a baking tray and bake for 5 minutes, or until golden. Leave to cool on a rack.

Mix the chives through the cottage cheese. Divide the lettuce, grapes and carrot between two lunchboxes, then arrange the cottage cheese and sprouts on top. Pack the lavash crisps separately so they don't become soggy, and eat them with the salad.

Makes 2 lunchbox salads

vietnamese salad with lemon grass dressing

burghul, feta and parsley salad

90 g (3¼ oz/½ cup) burghul
  (bulgar) wheat
2 tbs chopped flat-leaf (Italian)
  parsley
2 tbs chopped mint
4 spring onions (scallions),
  finely chopped

2 firm ripe tomatoes, halved,
  seeded and diced
1 short (Lebanese) cucumber,
  halved, seeded and diced
100 g (3½ oz) feta, crumbled
2 tbs lemon juice
2 tbs olive oil

Put the burghul in a large bowl and add enough hot water to cover. Leave to soak for 15–20 minutes, or until tender. Drain well, then thoroughly squeeze out all the excess liquid.

Gently toss the burghul in a bowl with all the remaining ingredients. Season with sea salt and freshly ground black pepper and mix together well. Divide between two lunchboxes and leave for at least an hour to allow all the flavours to mingle.

Makes 2 lunchbox salads

frisée salad with speck and croutons

vinaigrette
1/2 French shallot (eschalot),
    finely chopped
2 tsp Dijon mustard
1 1/2 tbs tarragon vinegar
4 tbs extra virgin olive oil

2 tsp olive oil
125 g (4 1/2 oz) speck, rind
    removed, cut into fine strips
1/4 baguette, sliced
2 garlic cloves
1/2 baby frisée (curly endive),
    washed and dried
50 g (3/4 oz/1/2 cup) toasted
    walnuts

To make the vinaigrette, whisk the shallot, mustard and vinegar in a small bowl. Slowly add the oil, whisking constantly until thickened. Set aside.

Heat the olive oil in a large frying pan. Add the speck, bread slices and whole garlic cloves and cook over medium heat for 5–8 minutes, or until the bread and speck are both crisp. Discard the garlic.

Arrange the speck in two lunchboxes with the frisée and walnuts. Pack the toasted bread slices separately so they stay crisp, and carry the vinaigrette separately so the lettuce doesn't become soggy. Just before eating, drizzle the vinaigrette over the salad and scatter with the croutons.

Makes 2 lunchbox salads

burghul, feta and parsley salad

A handful of nuts, some gourmet mushrooms and fresh, fiery
ginger turn plain noodles into a sumptuous lunchtime surprise.

buckwheat noodle salad with shiitake and snowpeas

125 g (4^1/$_2$ oz) buckwheat noodles
2 tbs walnut pieces
1 tbs vegetable or olive oil
60 g (2^1/$_4$ oz) fresh shiitake mushrooms, stalks discarded,
    caps thinly sliced
50 g (1^3/$_4$ oz/^{1}/$_2$ cup) snowpeas, tailed and finely sliced
3 spring onions (scallions), finely sliced

sesame ginger dressing
1 tbs white wine vinegar
^{1}/$_2$ tsp sesame oil
2 tbs vegetable oil
2 cm (^{3}/$_4$ inch) piece of ginger, peeled and finely grated
1 small red chilli, seeded and finely chopped

Cook the noodles according to the packet instructions. Drain well, then rinse under cold running water, rubbing the noodles together gently to remove some of the starch. Drain well, then place in a bowl.

Meanwhile, put a frying pan over high heat. Add the walnuts and dry-fry for 2–3 minutes, shaking the pan now and then so the nuts colour evenly. Remove, leave to cool and roughly chop.

Heat the oil in the same pan, add the mushrooms and sauté for about 2–3 minutes, or until tender. Add them to the noodles with the snowpeas, spring onion and chopped walnuts and gently mix together.

To make the sesame ginger dressing, put the vinegar, sesame oil and vegetable oil in a small bowl and whisk until well combined. Stir in the ginger and chilli, then drizzle over the noodles. Toss to combine, then divide the noodles between two lunchboxes. Eat at room temperature.

Makes 2 lunchbox salads

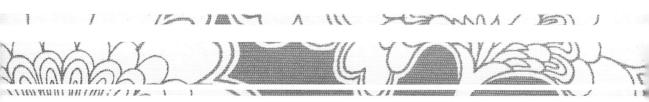

buckwheat noodle salad with shiitake and snowpeas

Zinging with lime, fresh herbs and chilli, this wonderful salad is a true pick-me-up after a dull morning.

chicken noodle salad

100 g (3¹/₂ oz) bean vermicelli noodles
1 tbs vegetable oil
1 garlic clove, crushed
3 cm (1¹/₄ inch) piece of fresh ginger, peeled and finely grated
1 green chilli, seeded and finely chopped
250 g (9 oz) minced (ground) chicken thighs
2 tbs lemon juice
2 makrut (kaffir lime) leaves, shredded
1 tbs fish sauce
1 tbs chilli sauce
2 tbs chopped coriander (cilantro) leaves

Put the noodles in a large heatproof bowl, cover with boiling water and soak for 5 minutes, or until softened. Alternatively, cook the noodles according to the packet instructions. Drain the noodles well, then rinse under cold water and drain again.

Heat the oil in a wok or frying pan over medium heat. Add the garlic, ginger and chilli and stir-fry for about 1 minute, being careful not to burn the garlic. Add the chicken and stir-fry for another 2–3 minutes. Stir in the lemon juice, lime leaves, fish sauce and chilli sauce and stir-fry for a further minute. Remove from the heat and transfer to a large bowl.

Cut the noodles into shorter lengths with scissors. Add to the chicken mixture along with the coriander and mix well. Leave to cool completely, then divide between two lunchboxes.

Makes 2 lunchbox salads

chicken noodle salad

caesar salad

dressing
1 egg
1 garlic clove, crushed
1 anchovy fillet
1/4 tsp Worcestershire sauce
3 tsp lime juice
1/2 tsp Dijon mustard
185 ml (6 fl oz/3/4 cup) olive oil

10 g (1/4 oz) butter
2 tsp olive oil
1 slice thick white bread, crust
    removed, cut into cubes
1 rasher of back bacon or
    rindless middle bacon
2 baby cos (romaine) lettuces,
    leaves washed and torn
35 g (11/4 oz/1/3 cup) shaved
    Parmesan cheese

To make the dressing, blend the egg, garlic, anchovy, Worcestershire sauce, lime juice and mustard in a food processor until smooth. With the motor running, add the oil in a thin, steady stream until creamy. Season well.

Heat the butter and oil in a frying pan. Fry the bread over medium heat until crisp, about 5–8 minutes, then remove. Cook the bacon in the same pan for 3 minutes or until crispy, then break into bite-sized pieces.

Divide the lettuce between two lunchboxes and scatter with the Parmesan. Pack the dressing in a separate container, and the bacon and croutons in another container. Add them to the salad just before eating.

Makes 2 lunchbox salads

chicken, pear and pasta salad

125 g (4¹/2 oz) gemelli, fusilli
   or other spiral pasta
100 g (3¹/2 oz) chicken breast
   fillet
1 pear, cored and thinly sliced
2 spring onions (scallions), finely
   sliced, plus extra, to serve

1 tbs toasted slivered almonds
50 g (1³/4 oz) creamy blue
   cheese
1¹/2 tbs sour cream

Cook the pasta in a large pot of rapidly boiling salted water until al dente. Drain, rinse under cold water and drain again. Allow to cool.

Put the chicken in a frying pan, cover with cold water and simmer gently for 8 minutes, or until tender, turning occasionally. Remove from the pan, allow to cool, then slice finely and place in a bowl with the cooled pasta. Add the pear, spring onion and almonds.

Put the blue cheese and sour cream in a food processor with a large pinch each of salt and pepper and 1¹/2 tablespoons of ice-cold water. Blend until smooth. Pour the mixture over the salad and gently toss to coat. Divide between two lunchboxes and scatter with a few slivers of spring onion.

Makes 2 lunchbox salads

Caramelized leek and lightly melted crumbs of creamy blue cheese lend a savoury sophistication to this simple pasta dish.

pasta salad with caramelized vegetables

2 tbs olive oil
2 celery stalks, sliced
1 small onion, halved and
   thinly sliced
1 garlic clove, crushed
pinch of sugar
2 leeks, white part only, sliced
175 g (6 oz) pasta shells or
   bows (see Note)
2 tbs toasted pine nuts

70 g (2^1/$_2$ oz) soft blue cheese,
   such as gorgonzola, crumbled

dressing
1 tbs olive oil
1 tbs chopped flat-leaf (Italian)
   parsley
1 tbs lemon juice

Heat the oil in a frying pan. Add the celery and onion, then cover and cook over medium heat for 5 minutes, stirring occasionally. Stir in the garlic, sugar and leek. Reduce the heat, cover the pan and gently cook, stirring occasionally, for a further 10 minutes, or until the vegetables are golden brown and soft. Remove the lid, increase the heat and cook the vegetables for another 2–3 minutes or until light golden, being careful not to burn them. Season with salt and black pepper, then set aside.

Meanwhile, cook the pasta in a large pot of rapidly boiling salted water until al dente. Drain well, then while the pasta is still warm, add the caramelized vegetables and set aside.

Put the dressing ingredients in a small bowl, season with salt and black pepper and mix well. Pour over the pasta, stir in the pine nuts and cheese and toss gently. Leave to cool, then divide between two lunchboxes. This salad is delicious cold, or equally delicious warmed up in a microwave.

Note: To save time, you could use 385 g (13^1/$_2$ oz/about 2^1/$_4$ cups) of cooked left-over pasta instead.

Makes 2 lunchbox salads

pasta salad with caramelized vegetables

warm winter   Long cold evenings and chilly weekends stoke up the appetite for good square meals that will warm you up without weighing you down. So when the mercury starts dropping, fire up

your enthusiasm and head straight for the kitchen. Whip on your apron, crank up your creativity, rustle up a wonderful warm salad and before long you'll feel a glow of contentment from top to toe.

The concept of cold and raw may be refreshing and appealing when the temperature is soaring and eating can seem a chore. But as the nights draw in ever earlier and you find yourself ferreting for last year's jumpers and thick woolly socks it takes a little something extra to make a satisfying meal. Roasts, stews and bakes naturally have their place in any winter repertoire, but satisfying doesn't have to mean stodgy. Weekend lunches, dinner for one and late-night meals after a long day at work are the prime times when many of us sneak off to the nearest takeaway shop or settle for the short-lived comfort of baked beans on toast in front of the television. But when preparing a full-blown meal seems off-putting and it's tempting to take to the couch and reach for the phone to order a lard-laden home delivery, don't despair: this is when the warm salad comes into its own. Healthy rather than worthy, the best warm salads take the finest produce of the season and turn winter's harvest into delectable, satisfying meals that nourish the soul as well as the body. Comfort food comes in all shapes and sizes and warm salads deserve to figure highly on the list. This is seriously good food that needn't involve an assembly line of ingredients and cooks. Warm, salty prosciutto, oozy melted cheese and fresh, delicate greens are all the more enticing when quickly cooked. Roasting root vegetables, onions and garlic brings a mellow warmth and caramelized sweetness that is infinitely soothing on a cold, dark evening — and as an added bonus, the hot oven turns a cold house into a cosy cocoon filled with heartening aromas. So it's time to welcome in food that is deeply invigorating — a celebration of winter and the opportunity for reflection and quiet contemplation that it brings.

scallop salad with lime and ginger

dressing
3 tbs peanut oil
1 tbs lime juice
1 tbs grated fresh ginger
$1/2$ tsp honey
1 tbs chopped coriander
   (cilantro)

3 zucchini (courgettes), julienned
2 carrots, julienned
2 spring onions (scallions),
   sliced on the diagonal
400 g (14 oz) scallops,
   without roe
1 tbs peanut oil

Put all the dressing ingredients in a small screw-top jar and shake well. Arrange the zucchini, carrot and spring onion on four serving plates.

Slice or pull off any vein, membrane or hard white muscle from the scallops. Rinse the scallops and pat them dry with paper towels.

Heat the oil in a heavy-based pan. Add the scallops and cook in small batches over high heat for 1 minute on each side, or until golden. Remove from the pan and keep warm while cooking the remaining batches.

Pile the scallops over the vegetables, drizzle with the dressing and serve.

Serves 4

thai-style chicken salad

4 chicken breast fillets, cut
    into 1 cm (1/2 inch) strips
1 tsp grated fresh ginger
1 garlic clove, crushed
2 tbs soy sauce
1 tbs peanut oil
3 spring onions (scallions),
    sliced diagonally

2 carrots, julienned
35 g (1¼ oz) snowpea
    (mangetout) sprouts

dressing
2 tbs sweet chilli sauce
1 tbs rice vinegar
2 tbs peanut oil

Put the chicken in a non-metallic dish. Mix together the ginger, garlic and soy sauce and smother the mixture all over the chicken. Cover and refrigerate for at least 2 hours — preferably overnight — turning occasionally.

Nearer to serving time, put all the dressing ingredients in a small screw-top jar and shake well.

Heat the oil in a heavy-based pan. Add the chicken and cook in batches over medium heat for 3–4 minutes, or until cooked and nicely browned. Drain on crumpled paper towels and set aside to cool, then place in a serving bowl with the spring onion, carrot and snowpea sprouts. Pour the dressing over the top and toss lightly to combine. Serve immediately.

Serves 4

thai-style chicken salad

spinach salad with bacon and quail eggs

12 quail eggs
2¹/₂ tbs oil
4 rashers of back bacon or
    middle rashers, cut into
    thin strips
2 tbs apple cider vinegar
2 garlic cloves, crushed
1 tsp Dijon mustard

1 tsp maple syrup
¹/₂ tsp Worcestershire sauce
250 g (9 oz) baby English
    spinach leaves
200 g (7 oz) cherry tomatoes,
    halved
50 g (1³/₄ oz/¹/₃ cup) toasted
    pine nuts

Bring a small saucepan of water to the boil. Carefully add the quail eggs and simmer for 1¹/₂ minutes. Drain, then refresh under cold running water until cool. Carefully peel the eggs and cut them in half.

Heat a little of the oil in a non-stick frying pan. Add the bacon and gently cook for 5 minutes, or until crisp. Remove with tongs, leaving the oil behind, and drain on crumpled paper towels. Add the vinegar, garlic, mustard, maple syrup and Worcestershire sauce to the pan and gently swirl for 2 minutes, or until bubbling. Add the remaining oil and heat for 1 minute.

Layer the spinach, bacon, tomatoes and pine nuts in a salad bowl. Add the quail eggs, pour the warm dressing over, season to taste and serve.

Serves 4

ricotta toasts with pear and walnut salad

1 small baguette, cut into
   16 thin slices
oil, for brushing
1 garlic clove, cut in half
100 g (3 1/2 oz/1 cup) walnuts
2 pears, cored and diced
2 tbs lime juice

400 g (14 oz) mixed salad leaves
200 g (7 oz) ricotta cheese

lime vinaigrette
3 tbs lime juice
3 tbs oil
2 tbs raspberry vinegar

Preheat the oven to 180°C (350°F/Gas 4). Brush the bread with a little oil, rub with the cut sides of the garlic, spread on a baking tray and bake for 10 minutes, or until golden. Bake the walnuts for 5 minutes, or until lightly browned, turning to ensure even colouring. Cool for 5 minutes.

Whisk the lime vinaigrette ingredients in a small bowl with 1 teaspoon salt and 1/2 teaspoon freshly ground black pepper. Put the pear cubes in a bowl, add the lime juice and mix well. Add the vinaigrette, salad leaves and walnuts, toss well, then divide between four serving bowls.

Spread the bread toasts with ricotta and cook under a hot griller (broiler) for 2–3 minutes, or until hot. Arrange four slices on each plate and serve.

Serves 4

spinach salad with bacon and quail eggs

mixed salad with warm brie dressing

1/2 sourdough baguette
165 ml (5³/4 fl oz) olive oil
6 rashers of streaky bacon
2 garlic cloves, peeled
2 baby cos (romaine) lettuces,
    leaves separated
90 g (3¹/4 oz/2 cups) baby
    English spinach leaves

80 g (2³/4 oz/¹/2 cup) toasted
    pine nuts
2 French shallots (eschalots),
    finely chopped
1 tbs Dijon mustard
4 tbs sherry vinegar
300 g (10¹/2 oz) ripe Brie
    cheese, rind removed

Preheat the oven to 180°C (350°F/Gas 4). Thinly slice the baguette and brush each slice all over with some of the oil. Spread on a baking tray and bake for 20 minutes, or until golden. Bake the bacon on a separate tray for 4 minutes, or until crisp, then break into pieces and leave to cool.

Rub the top of each toasted bread slice with one garlic clove, cut in half. Toss in a large bowl with the bacon, lettuce, spinach and pine nuts.

Heat the remaining oil in a frying pan. Add the shallot and gently cook for 1–2 minutes to soften. Crush the remaining garlic clove and add to the pan with the mustard and vinegar. Gently whisk in the Brie until it has melted. Pour the warm dressing over the salad, toss gently and serve.

Serves 4

roasted tomato, bacon and pasta salad

375 g (13 oz) cherry tomatoes
6 garlic cloves, unpeeled
2 tbs olive oil
400 g (14 oz) pasta
6 rashers (about 125 g/4$^{1}/_2$ oz)
   of rindless smoked bacon

150 g (5$^{1}/_2$ oz) feta cheese,
   crumbled
80 g (2$^{3}/_4$ oz/$^{1}/_2$ cup) Kalamata
   olives
1 large handful shredded basil

Preheat the oven to 180°C (350°F/Gas 4). Put the tomatoes and garlic in a roasting dish and drizzle with the oil. Season, toss lightly to coat, then bake for 15–20 minutes (reserve the roasting juices). Meanwhile, cook the pasta in a large pot of rapidly boiling salted water until al dente. Drain well.

Put a non-stick frying pan over high heat. Add the bacon and cook for 4–5 minutes, or until crispy. Remove the bacon with tongs, leaving all the pan juices behind, then chop into strips. Swish some of the pasta around the frying pan to soak up all the pan juices. Season with salt and pepper if needed, then empty into a large serving bowl with the rest of the pasta, the bacon, roasted tomatoes, feta and olives. Toss gently.

Squeeze the garlic cloves from their skins and mix them with the roasted tomato juices. Toss through the pasta, scatter with basil and serve warm.

Serves 4

roasted tomato, bacon and pasta salad

The distinctive peppery notes of horseradish, watercress and black pepper strike a sterling chord with subtle, salty salmon.

pepper-crusted salmon salad

1 tbs coarsely ground black pepper
4 salmon fillets (about 180 g/6 oz each), skin removed
80 g ($2^3/4$ oz/$1/3$ cup) ready-made mayonnaise
$1^1/2$ tbs lemon juice
2 tsp creamed horseradish
1 small garlic clove, crushed
2 tbs chopped parsley
100 g ($3^1/2$ oz/3 heaped cups) picked watercress
3 tbs olive oil
25 g (1 oz) butter
8 butter lettuce leaves, torn

Mix the pepper in a bowl with $1/4$ teaspoon salt. Use the mixture to coat both sides of each salmon fillet, pressing the pepper down firmly with your fingers. Cover and refrigerate for 30 minutes.

Put the mayonnaise in a food processor with the lemon juice, horseradish, garlic, parsley, half the watercress, 1 tablespoon of the oil and 1 tablespoon of warm water. Blend for 1 minute.

Heat the butter and 1 tablespoon of the oil in a large frying pan until bubbling. Add the salmon fillets and cook over medium heat for about 2–3 minutes on each side for medium-rare, or until cooked to your liking. Remove from the pan and allow to cool slightly.

Arrange the lettuce in the middle of four serving plates and drizzle lightly with the remaining oil. Break each salmon fillet into four pieces and arrange over the lettuce. Scatter the watercress over the top, pour the dressing over and serve at once.

Serves 4

pepper-crusted salmon salad

warm prawn, rocket and feta salad

3 spring onions (scallions)
3 Roma (plum) tomatoes
1 small red capsicum
   (pepper)
400 g (14 oz) tin chickpeas,
   rinsed and drained
1/2 tbs chopped dill
2 tbs finely shredded basil
2 tbs olive oil
40 g (11/2 oz) butter

750 g (1 lb 10 oz) raw prawns
   (shrimp), peeled and
   deveined, tails intact
1 small red chilli, finely chopped
3 garlic cloves, crushed
11/2 tbs lemon juice
200 g (7 oz/2 small bunches)
   rocket (arugula), trimmed
100 g (31/2 oz) feta cheese,
   crumbled

Chop the spring onion, tomato and capsicum and place in a bowl with the chickpeas, dill and basil. Toss well.

Heat the oil and butter in a large frying pan. Add the prawns and cook, stirring, over high heat for 2 minutes. Add the chilli and garlic and continue cooking until the prawns turn pink. Remove from the heat and stir in the lemon juice.

Arrange the rocket on a large platter and top with the tomato mixture, then the prawn mixture. Scatter with the crumbled feta and serve.

Serves 4

mini meatballs with couscous and yoghurt

600 g (1 lb 5 oz) lean minced
    (ground) beef
1 tsp chilli flakes
1 tsp ground cumin
2 tbs chopped pitted black olives
1 small onion, grated
2 tbs tomato paste (purée)
3–4 tbs olive oil

310 g (11 oz) instant couscous
250 g (9 oz/1 punnet) cherry
    tomatoes, halved
100 g (3½ oz) roasted red
    capsicum (pepper), diced
200 g (7 oz) thick plain yoghurt
2 tbs lemon juice
2 tbs chopped parsley

Put the beef, chilli flakes, cumin, olives, onion and tomato paste in a bowl. Season, mix well with your hands and roll into 40 balls. Chill for 30 minutes.

Put 275 ml (9½ fl oz) water in a saucepan with 2 tablespoons of the oil and 2 teaspoons of salt. Bring to the boil, remove from the heat and add the couscous. Stir, then cover and leave to stand for 2–3 minutes. Fluff up with a fork and add the tomatoes and capsicum. Season and mix well.

Heat the remaining oil in a large frying pan. Fry the meatballs over medium heat for 10–12 minutes, or until cooked through, then arrange them over the couscous. Mix the yoghurt, lemon juice and parsley together with 1 tablespoon water, drizzle over the meatballs and serve.

Serves 4

mini meatballs with couscous and yoghurt

pumpkin and prawn salad with rocket

800 g (1 lb 10 oz) pumpkin,
    peeled and cut into
    3 cm (1¼ inch) cubes
2 small red onions, cut
    into thick wedges
1 tbs oil
2 cloves garlic, crushed

500 g (10½ oz) cooked
    prawns (shrimp), peeled
    and deveined
200 g (7 oz) baby rocket
    (arugula) leaves
1–2 tbs balsamic vinegar
1 tbs olive oil

Preheat the oven to 200°C (400°F/Gas 6). Toss the pumpkin and onion in a large bowl with the oil and garlic. Spread in a single layer on a baking tray and bake for 25–30 minutes, or until tender. Transfer to a serving bowl, add the prawns and rocket and gently toss together.

Whisk together the vinegar and oil, and season to taste with sea salt and freshly ground black pepper. Drizzle over the salad and serve.

Serves 4

mussel salad with warm saffron dressing

500 g (1 lb 2 oz) new potatoes
1 kg (2 lb 4 oz) black mussels
170 ml (5^1/$_2$ fl oz/^{2}/$_3$ cup) dry
   white wine
1 small onion, sliced

2 thyme sprigs
2 fresh or dried bay leaves
large pinch of powdered saffron
4 tbs sour cream
2 tsp chopped parsley

Cook the potatoes in salted boiling water until tender. Drain and leave to cool slightly. Meanwhile, scrub the mussels with a stiff brush and pull out the hairy beards. Discard any broken mussels, or open ones that don't close when tapped on the bench. Rinse well under running water.

Put the wine, onion, thyme, bay leaves and half the mussels in a pot. Cover and cook over high heat, stirring once, for 3–4 minutes, or until the mussels start to open. Remove the mussels as they open and discard any unopened ones. Cook the remaining mussels and leave to cool slightly. Strain the mussel stock, reserving 125 ml (4 fl oz/^{1}/$_2$ cup). While the liquid is still warm, stir in the saffron. Whisk in the sour cream and season well.

Quarter any large potatoes and halve the small ones. Remove the mussels from their shells, place in a serving bowl with the potatoes and gently mix the warm saffron dressing through. Sprinkle with the parsley and serve.

Serves 4

pumpkin and prawn salad with rocket

mushroom and shredded chicken salad

1–2 tbs olive oil
200 g (7 oz) small button
   mushrooms
200 g (7 oz) other mixed
   mushrooms (such as Swiss
   brown and shiitake), larger
   ones halved or quartered
400 g (14 oz) cooked chicken,
   shredded
200 g (7 oz) mixed salad leaves

lime and soy dressing
2 tbs lime juice
1 tbs soy sauce
2 tbs olive oil
1 tbs sweet chilli sauce
1 tbs red wine vinegar

Heat 1 tablespoon of the oil in a frying pan. Add the mushrooms and cook over medium heat for 2–3 minutes, or until softened. Toss in a large bowl with the shredded chicken.

Combine all the lime and soy dressing ingredients in a small bowl or jug, mix well and pour two-thirds over the warm mushrooms.

Arrange the salad leaves in a serving dish and toss through the remaining dressing. Top with the chicken and mushrooms and serve warm.

Serves 4

warm chicken and pasta salad

375 g (13 oz) penne
125 ml (4 fl oz/1/2 cup) olive oil
4 slender eggplants (aubergines), thinly sliced on the diagonal
2 chicken breast fillets
2 tsp lemon juice
2 handfuls parsley, chopped
270 g (9 3/4 oz) chargrilled red capsicum (pepper) slices
175 g (7 oz/1 bunch) asparagus spears, trimmed and blanched
85 g (3 oz) semi-dried (sun-blushed) tomatoes, sliced
grated Parmesan cheese, to serve

Cook the pasta in a large pot of rapidly boiling salted water until al dente. Drain, return to the pan and keep warm.

Meanwhile, heat 2 tablespoons of the oil in a large frying pan. Fry the eggplant over high heat for 4–5 minutes, or until golden and cooked through; remove. Heat another 2 tablespoons of oil in the pan, reduce the heat to medium and cook the chicken for 4–5 minutes on each side, or until lightly browned and cooked through. Allow to cool, then thickly slice.

Put the remaining oil in a small screw-top jar with the lemon juice and parsley and shake well. Return the pasta to the heat and toss through the dressing, chicken, eggplant, capsicum, asparagus and tomato to warm through. Season with black pepper, scatter with Parmesan and serve.

Serves 4

mushroom and shredded chicken salad

squid and scallops with chermoula dressing

8 baby squid, cleaned and rinsed
200 g (7 oz) scallops, without roe
2 tbs oil
150 g (5 1/2 oz/1 bunch) rocket
   (arugula), trimmed
3 ripe Roma (plum) tomatoes,
   chopped
2 oranges, peeled and
   segmented

chermoula dressing
4 large handfuls coriander
   (cilantro), finely chopped
2 1/2 large handfuls flat-leaf
   (Italian) parsley, chopped
2 tsp ground cumin
1 tsp ground paprika
3 tbs lime juice
3 tbs olive oil

Put the squid in a bowl of water with 1/4 teaspoon salt. Mix well, then chill for 30 minutes. Drain well, then cut the tubes into long thin strips and the tentacles into pieces. Rinse the scallops and pat them dry with paper towels.

Heat the oil in a large deep frying pan. Cook the squid in batches over high heat for 1 minute, or until they turn white. Remove and drain. Fry the scallops in small batches over high heat for 1 minute on each side, until golden.

Arrange the rocket on a large platter, then top with the seafood, tomato and orange segments. Quickly whisk the chermoula dressing ingredients together in a non-metallic bowl, pour over the seafood and serve.

Serves 4

warm pasta and crab salad

300 g (10¹/2 oz) thin spaghetti
2 tbs olive oil
20 g (³/4 oz) butter, chopped
350 g (12 oz) fresh crab meat
1 red capsicum (pepper), cut
    into thin strips

1¹/2 tsp finely grated lemon zest
3 tbs grated Parmesan cheese
2 tbs snipped chives
3 tbs chopped parsley

Break all the spaghetti in half and cook in a large pot of rapidly boiling salted water until al dente. Drain well, then place in a large serving bowl and toss with the oil and butter.

Add the crab meat, capsicum, lemon zest, Parmesan, chives and parsley, and toss to combine. Sprinkle with freshly ground black pepper and serve.

Serves 4

warm pasta and crab salad

minced pork and noodle salad

1 tbs peanut oil
500 g (1 lb 2 oz) minced
    (ground) pork
2 garlic cloves, finely chopped
1 stem lemon grass, white
    part only, finely chopped
3 red Asian shallots, finely sliced
3 tsp finely grated fresh ginger
1 small red chilli, finely chopped
5 makrut (kaffir lime) leaves,
    very finely shredded
170 g (6 oz) glass (mung bean)
    noodles

60 g (2¹/₄ oz) baby English
    spinach leaves
4 large handfuls coriander
    (cilantro), chopped
1 large handful mint leaves

dressing
1¹/₂ tbs grated palm sugar
    or soft brown sugar
2 tbs fish sauce
4 tbs lime juice
2 tsp sesame oil
2 tsp peanut oil

Heat a wok until very hot, add the oil and swirl to coat. Stir-fry the pork in batches over high heat for 5 minutes, or until golden. Add the garlic, lemon grass, shallot, ginger, chilli and lime leaves and stir-fry until fragrant.

Cover the noodles with boiling water to soften. Rinse, drain and toss in a bowl with the pork, spinach, coriander and mint. Whisk together the dressing ingredients and toss through the salad. Season with pepper and serve.

Serves 4

roasted vegetables with pan-fried garlic breadcrumbs

3 zucchini (courgettes), sliced

225 g (8 oz) button mushrooms, larger ones halved

1 red onion, cut into 8 wedges

1 red capsicum (pepper), diced

3 tbs olive oil

1 garlic clove, crushed

40 g (1½ oz/½ cup) breadcrumbs, made from day-old bread

dressing

1 tbs olive oil

2 tbs ready-made pesto

1 tbs lemon juice

Preheat the oven to 200°C (400°F/Gas 6). Put all the vegetables in a large baking dish. Drizzle over 2 tablespoons of the oil, add a little salt and pepper and shake the pan to coat all the vegetables in the oil. Roast for 30 minutes, or until all the vegetables are tender.

Combine the dressing ingredients in a large serving bowl. Add the roasted vegetables, toss gently and leave for 10 minutes for the flavours to absorb.

Heat the remaining oil in a frying pan and fry the garlic over medium heat for about 30 seconds. Increase the heat, add the breadcrumbs and fry for 2–3 minutes, or until golden, shaking the pan and stirring the crumbs. Toss the toasted breadcrumbs through the salad and serve.

Serves 4

roasted vegetables with pan-fried garlic breadcrumbs

warm mixed bean salad

2 tbs olive oil
125 ml (4 fl oz/1/2 cup) tomato
    juice
2 tbs chopped flat-leaf (Italian)
    parsley
pinch of sugar
3 garlic cloves

400 g (14 oz) tin borlotti beans,
    drained and rinsed
400 g (14 oz) tin cannellini
    beans, drained and rinsed
2 tomatoes, diced
4 thick slices crusty bread

Put 1 tablespoon of the oil in a small bowl with the tomato juice, parsley and sugar. Crush two of the garlic cloves and stir them into the mixture.

Put the borlotti and cannellini beans in a frying pan, add the tomato mixture and place over medium heat for about 5 minutes, or until well warmed through. Toss through the diced tomato and season to taste.

Meanwhile, toast the bread slices. Cut the remaining garlic clove and rub the cut side all over the bread. Drizzle with the remaining oil and serve hot with the warm beans.

Serves 4

warm lentil and rice salad

185 ml (6 fl oz/3/4 cup) olive oil
30 g (1 oz) butter
3 large red onions, finely sliced
3 garlic cloves, crushed
2 tsp ground cinnamon
2 tsp ground sweet paprika
2 tsp ground cumin

2 tsp ground coriander
140 g (5 oz/3/4 cup) green lentils
150 g (5 1/2 oz/3/4 cup) basmati
   rice
3 spring onions (scallions),
   finely chopped

Heat the oil and butter in a frying pan. When the butter has melted, add the onion and garlic and cook over low heat, stirring, for 30 minutes, or until very soft. Stir in the cinnamon, paprika, cumin and ground coriander and cook for a few minutes longer, or until aromatic. Keep warm.

Meanwhile, bring a pot of water to the boil, add the rice and cook until the grains are just tender. While the rice is cooking, bring another pot of water to the boil, add the lentils and cook until just tender.

Drain the rice and lentils well, then transfer to a large serving bowl and mix through the onion mixture, spring onion and freshly ground black pepper to taste. Serve warm.

Serves 4

warm mixed bean salad

warm thai tuna salad

650 g (1 lb 7 oz) fresh tuna steaks
1 tbs olive oil
2 tbs oyster sauce
2 tbs soy sauce
2 tbs lime juice
300 g (10$\frac{1}{2}$ oz) dried egg noodles
125 g (4$\frac{1}{2}$ oz) baby corn, halved
150 g (5$\frac{1}{2}$ oz) snowpeas
   (mangetout), tailed

coriander chilli dressing

2 tbs fish sauce
2 tbs lime juice
2 tbs Thai sweet chilli sauce
2 tbs vegetable oil
1 small red chilli, chopped
3 tbs chopped coriander
   (cilantro)

Put the tuna in a shallow dish in a single layer. Whisk together the oil, oyster sauce, soy sauce and lime juice and pour the mixture over the tuna, turning to coat all over. Cover and refrigerate for 30 minutes.

Cook the noodles according to the packet instructions, adding the corn and snowpeas for the final 45 seconds. Drain well, then toss in a serving bowl. Combine the dressing ingredients and mix half through the noodles.

Heat a chargrill pan (griddle) to high. Cook the tuna for 3–4 minutes on each side, so it's still pink in the middle. Cool slightly, then slice into strips. Serve separately or over the noodles, with the remaining dressing on the side.

Serves 4

salmon and green bean salad

2 tsp olive oil
275 g (9³/4 oz) salmon fillet,
 skin removed
vegetable oil, for deep-frying
3 garlic cloves, thinly sliced
150 g (5¹/2 oz) white sweet
 potato, thinly sliced
75 g (2¹/2 oz) green beans,
 trimmed and blanched
1 small red onion, thinly sliced

1 tbs toasted sesame seeds
1 mizuna lettuce, leaves torn

lime and tahini dressing
2 garlic cloves, crushed
1¹/2 tbs tahini
3 tsp rice vinegar
1¹/2 tbs lime juice
3 tsp soy sauce
2 tbs olive oil

Heat the oil in a frying pan. Cook the salmon over medium heat for
2–3 minutes on each side. Cool slightly, then cut into chunks.

Fill a deep-fryer or wok one-third full of oil and heat to 180°C (350°F), or
until a cube of bread dropped in the oil browns in 15 seconds. In separate
batches, cook the garlic and sweet potato until golden and crisp, then drain.

Whisk together the dressing ingredients. Toss the garlic and sweet potato
in a bowl with the beans, onion, sesame seeds and lettuce. Divide between
four serving plates, top with salmon, drizzle with the dressing and serve.

Serves 4

warm thai tuna salad

index

A

arugula *see* rocket
Asian dressing 56
Asian pork salad 113
Asian salmon salad 56
Asian tofu salad 112
asparagus
   chicken and spring vegetable
     salad 100
   haloumi and asparagus salad
     with salsa verde 117
   smoked trout with chilli
     raspberry dressing 88
   warm chicken and pasta salad
     183
aubergine *see* eggplant
avocado
   avocado, bacon and tomato
     salad 120
   avocado and black bean
     salad 36
   goat's cheese, avocado and
     smoked salmon salad 20

B

bacon
   avocado, bacon and tomato
     salad 120
   Caesar salad 148
   frisée salad with speck and
     croutons 137

mixed salad with warm brie
   dressing 166
roasted tomato, bacon and
   pasta salad 167
spinach salad with bacon and
   quail eggs 162
beans
   avocado and black bean salad
     36
   borlotti bean, beetroot and
     mint salad 97
   chicken and spring vegetable
     salad 100
   salmon and green bean salad
     199
   south-western black bean
     salad 85
   three-bean salad 48
   warm mixed bean salad 194
beef
   mini meatballs with couscous
     and yoghurt 175
   roast beef and spinach salad
     with horseradish cream 24
   Thai beef salad 76
beetroot
   beetroot and chive salad 129
   borlotti bean, beetroot and
     mint salad 97
black beans
   avocado and black bean salad
     36
   south-western black bean
     salad 85
broccoli with grilled tofu and
   sesame dressing 32

buckwheat noodle salad with
   shiitake and snowpeas 140
burghul, feta and parsley salad
   136

C

Caesar salad 148
caramel
   caramelized onion and potato
     salad 125
   pasta salad with caramelized
     vegetables 150
carrot salad, Moroccan spiced 29
cheese
   burghul, feta and parsley
     salad 136
   Caesar salad 148
   chicken, pear and pasta salad 149
   cottage cheese salad 133
   goat's cheese, avocado and
     smoked salmon salad 20
   grilled haloumi salad with
     herb dressing 60
   haloumi and asparagus salad
     with salsa verde 117
   insalata caprese 28
   mixed salad with warm brie
     dressing 166
   pasta salad with caramelized
     vegetables 150
   ricotta toasts with pear and
     walnut salad 163
   roasted tomato, bacon and
     pasta salad 167
   tomato and bocconcini salad
     124

warm prawn, rocket and feta
    salad 174
chermoula 186
chicken
    chicken, pear and pasta salad
        149
    chicken with green chilli salsa
        verde 52
    chicken noodle salad 144
    chicken and spring vegetable
        salad 100
    chilli chicken and cashew
        salad 121
    mushroom and shredded
        chicken salad 182
    roast cherry tomato and
        chicken salad 89
    Thai-style chicken salad 159
    warm chicken and pasta
        salad 183
chickpeas, warm prawn, rocket
    and feta salad 174
chilli
    chicken with green chilli salsa
        verde 52
    chicken noodle salad 144
    chilli chicken and cashew
        salad 121
    marinated fish salad with chilli
        and basil 93
    roast duck salad with chilli
        dressing 72
    smoked trout with chilli
        raspberry dressing 88
coconut

crab salad with green mango
    and coconut 80
marinated fish salad with chilli
    and basil 93
coriander chilli dressing 198
cottage cheese salad 133
couscous
    mini meatballs with couscous
        and yoghurt 175
    pistachio couscous 44
crab
    crab salad with green mango
        and coconut 80
    warm pasta and crab
        salad 187
cucumber
    burghul, feta and parsley
        salad 136
    grilled haloumi salad with
        herb dressing 60
curly endive see frisée

D

dressings
    Asian 56
    chermoula 186
    chilli 72
    chilli raspberry 88
    coriander chilli 198
    ginger and chilli 113
    herb 60
    horseradish cream 24
    Japanese 104
    lemon and Dijon 73
    lemon grass 132
    lemon mayonnaise 125

lemon tarragon 100
lime and chilli 36
lime and soy 182
lime and tahini 199
lime vinaigrette 163
mint 128
mint and chilli 76
sake 68
sesame 32, 105
sesame ginger 140
vinaigrette 137
duck salad, roast, with chilli
    dressing 72

E

eggplant, warm chicken and
    pasta salad 183
eggs
    Caesar salad 148
    spinach salad with bacon and
        quail eggs 162

F

farfalle salad with sun-dried
    tomatoes and spinach 116
fennel
    prawn and fennel salad 73
    red leaf salad 33
feta
    burghul, feta and parsley
        salad 136
    roasted tomato, bacon and
        pasta salad 167
    warm prawn, rocket and feta
        salad 174

figs with radicchio and ginger
vinaigrette 37
fish *see* seafood
frisée salad with speck and
croutons 137

G

garden salad 96
garlic
garlic breadcrumbs 191
roasted tomato and pasta
salad with pesto 49
ginger
chicken noodle salad 144
ginger and chilli dressing 113
radicchio with figs and ginger
vinaigrette 37
scallop, ginger and spinach
salad 68
scallop salad with lime and
ginger 158
goat's cheese, avocado and
smoked salmon salad 20
green chilli salsa verde 52

H

haloumi
grilled haloumi salad with
herb dressing 60
haloumi and asparagus salad
with salsa verde 117
harissa 45
herb dressing 60
horseradish cream 24

I

insalata caprese 28

J

Japanese dressing 104

L

lamb salad, Moroccan 44
lemon
lemon dressings 73, 100
lemon mayonnaise 125
lemon grass dressing 132
lentils
minty lentil salad 128
warm lentil and rice salad 195
lettuce
Caesar salad 148
cottage cheese salad 133
garden salad 96
mixed salad with warm brie
dressing 166
red leaf salad 33
lime
chicken noodle salad 144
chicken and spring vegetable
salad 100
lime dressings 36, 163, 182,
199
marinated fish salad with chilli
and basil 93
salmon and green bean
salad 199
scallop salad with lime and
ginger 158

M

mangetout *see* snowpeas
mango
crab salad with green mango
and coconut 80
marinated fish salad with chilli
and basil 93
seared Asian salmon salad 56
Vietnamese salad with lemon
grass dressing 132
mayonnaise, lemon 125
meatballs, mini, with couscous
and yoghurt 175
mint
borlotti bean, beetroot and
mint salad 97
mint and chilli dressing 77
mint dressing 128
minty lentil salad 128
Moroccan lamb salad 44
Moroccan spiced carrot
salad 29
mozzarella
insalata caprese 28
tomato and bocconcini salad 124
mushrooms
buckwheat noodle salad with
shiitake and snowpeas 140
mushroom and shredded
chicken salad 182
mussel salad with warm saffron
dressing 179

N

noodles

buckwheat noodle salad with
    shiitake and snowpeas 140
chicken noodle salad 144
minced pork and noodle salad
    190
prawn and rice noodle salad
    16
Thai noodle salad 92
Vietnamese salad with lemon
    grass dressing 132

O
octopus, marinated baby
octopus salad 21
onion
    caramelized onion and potato
        salad 125
    warm lentils and rice salad
        195

P
pasta
    chicken, pear and pasta salad
        149
    farfalle salad with sun-dried
        tomatoes and spinach 116
    pasta salad with caramelized
        vegetables 150
    roasted tomato, bacon and
        pasta salad 167
    roasted tomato and pasta
        salad with pesto 49
    warm chicken and pasta
        salad 183
    warm pasta and crab salad 187

pear
    chicken, pear and pasta salad
        149
    pear and sprout salad with
        sesame dressing 105
    ricotta toasts with pear and
        walnut salad 163
pepper-crusted salmon salad 170
pistachio couscous 44
pork
    Asian pork salad 113
    minced pork and noodle salad
        190
potato
    caramelized onion and potato
        salad 125
    mussel salad with warm
        saffron dressing 179
prawns
    prawn and fennel salad 73
    prawn and rice noodle salad
        16
    pumpkin and prawn salad with
        rocket 178
    Thai noodle salad 92
    Vietnamese prawn salad 69
    warm prawn, rocket and feta
        salad 174

R
radicchio with figs and ginger
    vinaigrette 37
red leaf salad 33
rice and lentil salad, warm 195
ricotta toasts with pear and
    walnut salad 163

rocket
    garden salad 96
    pumpkin and prawn salad
        with rocket 178
    tomato and bocconcini salad
        124
    warm prawn, rocket and feta
        salad 174

S
sake dressing 68
salmon
    goat's cheese, avocado and
        smoked salmon salad 20
    pepper-crusted salmon salad
        170
    salmon and green bean salad 199
    seared Asian salmon salad 56
salsa verde 40, 117
    green chilli 52
scallops
    scallop, ginger and spinach
        salad 68
    scallop salad with lime and
        ginger 158
squid and scallops with
    chermoula dressing 186
seafood
    crab salad with green mango
        and coconut 80
    goat's cheese, avocado and
        smoked salmon salad 20
    marinated baby octopus salad
        21
    marinated fish salad with chilli
        and basil 93

mussel salad with warm
saffron dressing 179
pepper-crusted salmon salad
170
salmon and green bean salad
199
scallop, ginger and spinach
salad 68
scallop salad with lime and
ginger 158
seared Asian salmon salad 56
smoked trout with chilli
raspberry dressing 88
squid salad with salsa verde 40
squid and scallops with
chermoula dressing 186
warm pasta and crab salad
187
warm Thai tuna salad 198
see also prawns
sesame dressings 32, 105, 140
shrimp see prawns
snowpeas
buckwheat noodle salad with
shiitake and snowpeas 140
snowpea salad with Japanese
dressing 104
Thai noodle salad 92
south-western black bean salad 85
spinach
farfalle salad with sun-dried
tomatoes and spinach 116
mixed salad with warm brie
dressing 166
roast beef and spinach salad
with horseradish cream 24

scallop, ginger and spinach
salad 68
spinach salad with bacon and
quail eggs 162
sprouts
Asian pork salad 113
Asian tofu salad 112
pear and sprout salad with
sesame dressing 105
seared Asian salmon salad 56
snowpea salad with Japanese
dressing 104
squid salad with salsa verde 40
squid and scallops with
chermoula dressing 186

T

Thai beef salad 76
Thai noodle salad 92
Thai tuna salad, warm 198
Thai-style chicken salad 159
three-bean salad 48
tofu
Asian tofu salad 112
grilled tofu with broccoli and
sesame dressing 32
tomato
avocado, bacon and tomato
salad 120
chargrilled tomato salad 84
farfalle salad with sun-dried
tomatoes and spinach 116
insalata caprese 28
mini meatballs with couscous
and yoghurt 175

roast cherry tomato and
chicken salad 89
roasted tomato, bacon and
pasta salad 167
roasted tomato and pasta
salad with pesto 49
tomato and bocconcini salad
124
trout, smoked, with chilli
raspberry dressing 88
tuna, warm Thai tuna salad 198

V

vegetables
chicken and spring vegetable
salad 100
pasta salad with caramelized
vegetables 150
roasted vegetables with
pan-fried garlic
breadcrumbs 191
Vietnamese prawn salad 69
Vietnamese salad with lemon
grass dressing 132
vinaigrette 137
ginger 37
lime 163

Y

yoghurt
mini meatballs with couscous
and yoghurt 175
Moroccan spiced carrot salad 29

Published in 2011 by Murdoch Books Pty Limited

Murdoch Books Australia
Pier 8/9, 23 Hickson Road
Millers Point NSW 2000
Phone: +61 (0)2 8220 2000
Fax: +61 (0)2 8220 2558
www.murdochbooks.com.au

Murdoch Books UK Limited
Erico House, 6th Floor
93–99 Upper Richmond Road
Putney, London SW15 2TG
Phone: +44 (0)20 8785 5995
Fax: +44 (0)20 8785 5985
www.murdochbooks.co.uk

Chief Executive: Juliet Rogers
Publishing Director: Chris Rennie

Publisher: Lynn Lewis
Senior Designer: Heather Menzies
Design Layout: Handpress Graphics
Editorial Coordinator: Liz Malcolm
Production: Joan Beal

National Library of Australia Cataloguing-in-Publication Data
Title: Salads. ISBN: 978-1-74196-946-7 (pbk.)
Series: New chubbie. Notes: Includes index. Subjects: Salads. Dewey Number: 641.83

Printed by 1010 Printing International.
PRINTED IN CHINA

IMPORTANT: Those who might be at risk from the effects of salmonella poisoning (the elderly, pregnant women, young children and those suffering from immune deficiency diseases) should consult their doctor with any concerns about eating raw eggs.

OVEN GUIDE: You may find cooking times vary depending on the oven you are using. For fan-forced ovens, as a general rule, set the oven temperature to 20°C (35°F) lower than indicated in the recipe.